PRAISE FOR

Conversations with the
Greatest Networker in the World

"I once wrote that John Milton Fogg would be recalled, in future years, in the same breath as Dale Carnegie, Norman Vincent Peale, and Napoleon Hill. His latest book, *Conversations with the Greatest Networker in the World*, has proven my point. Everyone who aspires to greatness must read this book."

—RICHARD POE,
author of *Wave 3* and
Wave 4: Network Marketing in the 21st Century

"*Conversations* . . . is the path to Mastery. Once again, Mr. Fogg illuminates the way of the MLM Warrior. Study it for life!

—RICHARD B. BROOKE,
president and CEO of Oxyfresh Worldwide
and author of *Mach II with Your Hair on Fire!*

"Fogg has done it again! Another brilliant, motivational work. Packed with information of real value. Get it and read it today!

—RANDY GAGE,
author of *How to Build a Multi-Level Money Machine*

"Most books teach *what* to believe. John Fogg is one of those remarkable people who teaches you *how* to believe. *Conversations with the Greatest Networker in the World* shows and tells anyone how you can build a rock-solid belief in your ability to be a great success in your life and work.

—TOM "BIG AL" SCHREITER,
author of the *Big Al* books

"John Fogg's *Conversations with the Greatest Networker in the World* gets right to the core of *who to be* for unlimited success. If you're planning to be a big winner in this industry, then you must not only read this book, but have your *entire* downline read it. This book is like being mentored by the man himself!

—KENTUCKY DOUGLAS,
founder and director of
The Young Networkers Association

CONVERSATIONS WITH

The
Greatest
Networker
in the World

MORE OF THE STORY...

John Milton Fogg

PRIMA PUBLISHING
3000 Lava Ridge Court • Roseville, California 95661
(800) 632-8676 • www.primalifestyles.com

PRIMA PUBLISHING and colophon are registered trademarks of Prima Communications, Inc.

Library of Congress Cataloging-in-Publication Data
Fogg, John Milton.
    Conversations with—the greatest networker in the world /
John Milton Fogg.
        p.   cm.
      ISBN 0-7615-2435-5
      1. Multilevel marketing. 2. Success—Psychological aspects.
    I. Fogg, John Milton. Greatest networker in the world.
    HF5415.126 .F63 2000
    158—dc21   99-059430

00 01 02 03 04 05 HH 10 9 8 7 6 5 4 3 2 1
Printed in the United States of America

HOW TO ORDER

Single copies may be ordered from Prima Publishing, 3000 Lava Ridge Court, Roseville, CA 95661; telephone (800) 632-8676. Quantity discounts are also available. On your letterhead, include information concerning the intended use of the books and the number of books you wish to purchase.

Visit us online at www.primalifestyles.com

This book is dedicated to you—
and you know who you are. . . .

Contents

More of the Story

DO YOU REMEMBER how *The Greatest Networker in the World* ended with "The Beginning"?

* * *

I TOLD YOU as I drove to the hotel for our weekly meeting that Thursday after work, that if someone would have told me beforehand the events that happened to me in just one brief week were going to happen, I would never ever have believed them. And I added that I was actually beginning to believe anything was possible.

Here, let me retell my ending/beginning for you.

* * *

"WHAT THE MIND can believe, you can achieve."

"Who said that?" I asked myself out loud. "Clement Stone . . . ? Napoleon Hill . . . ? Me . . . ?"

One thing was for certain: I was convinced that all you really needed to do was to begin to believe—and accomplishment after accomplishment would follow.

By the time I had returned home from The Greatest Networker's late Saturday night, I'd begun to balance every scale in my mind in my favor—forever.

The kids were asleep when I got in, but Kathy was up and we stayed awake 'til dawn talking . . . talking about my weekend, about my old beliefs and new beliefs, about what she believed and wanted to replace her old habits with. . . . We hadn't done anything remotely like that since we were dating.

Even though I was dead tired from lack of sleep, that Sunday was the most fantastic day. We went to a special place Kathy and I knew since we first arrived here. We hiked back up through the woods with the kids running around, then being carried, then running up and back the trail again. There was a pond we'd discovered long ago and we all went swimming—splashing about, throwing the kids up in the air . . . I cannot remember feeling so free . . . so relaxed . . . so at home with myself and my family.

We all went to that Italian restaurant where The Greatest Networker had taken me for dinner that night. The valet remembered me. The maître d' recognized me and said how it was so nice to see me again. Kathy looked at me and raised her eyebrows. I loved it!

Oh, and this you won't believe! Remember, I was the guy who hadn't sponsored a soul? Well, guess what? That week— three new people! That's right—three! And tonight, two of them were coming to the meeting, and each one was bringing a guest! No kidding.

That's not the best part. One of the people I sponsored— my boss! He'd come into my office the day before, just before lunch time. He said, "Man, I don't know what you're taking, but I want whatever it is now!" I laughed and told him, if he'd buy me lunch, I'd give him a year's worth. He signed up with me right then and there.

And it got even better. My boss said he'd been interested in Network Marketing for a number of years, but he'd heard some conflicting opinions about it and had never really understood it before I explained it. He told me he'd been a teacher right out of college, but the money wasn't any good, and what he really wanted to teach people was about how to succeed in life. "Network Marketing sounds perfect," he said to me. "How do I start?"

Amazing.

Everything was amazing.

The truth is, my life had changed 180 degrees in just five days.

* * *

I PULLED MY CAR up to the front entrance of the hotel. Chris, the doorman I had met the week before, came out and opened the car door before I'd turned the engine off.

I said hello to him and asked if he'd be willing to park my car behind that gray pickup truck, and he said he'd be glad to. I asked him if he was really serious about what he said about going to Japan, and he said he was. So I asked if we could have lunch or dinner and talk about that sometime. He said he'd love that, and we shook hands.

I walked into the hotel room, looking for my new people and their guests. There they were, early—with two more people than I'd expected! I became so engrossed in talking with them and asking them questions that I didn't notice the man standing beside me—until, at a break in the conversation, I heard a familiar voice say, "Pardon me, I just wanted to say how great you looked."

I reached out my hand, but he brushed it aside and gave me a big hug, then held me away a little and looked at me. "You really look fantastic," he said. "How are you?"

"I'm even better than I look," I said, and there was more than a hint of sheer glee in my voice.

He nodded his head up and down and then laughed that patented booming laugh of his.

"I'll just bet!" he said, his smile growing even bigger.

"Meet my friends," I insisted, and he did.

I introduced him to them, and I could tell by the expressions on their faces that coming to their first meeting and being introduced to The Greatest Networker in the World was a tad more than they thought they'd signed on for. It was great! I stood back just a little as he welcomed them and began asking them questions. A couple of times he glanced over at me with an appreciative look and a nod as he learned that I had just sponsored them and how excited they were to be here.

It felt so great!

He turned to me and put one hand on my shoulder, "You are one very quick study, my friend."

"I've had a superb mentor," I replied.

"Thank you," he said, with genuine warmth and a squeeze on my shoulder. "Now," he said with a deep breath and a smile, "are you ready to surpass your teacher?"

I looked into his eyes. There was no expression I could read there—I knew there wouldn't be. I closed my eyes and took a deep breath. Images cascaded through my mind—vivid ones of me as a dynamic, capable, and powerful leader.

"Yes," I said, opening my eyes and looking back at him.

"Good," he said. "The meeting's starting. Let's sit down."

The meeting was one of the best I'd attended. (Had the meeting changed that much, or had I?) The energy was high, there was humor and laughter. It flew along from speaker to speaker and I could tell by the faces of my guests that they were finding it interesting and involving, too—and they were pleased they'd come.

At last, they introduced The Greatest Networker, to an immediate standing ovation speckled with cheers and whistles.

He stood in front of the group, acknowledging our applause. After we'd finished clapping and sat down, he remained standing there silently for a long time, just looking at us. He seemed to take in each and every face in the room.

At last, he spoke.

* * *

"TONIGHT, I AM going to show you the secret for success.

"Now, if you're listening very carefully, you noticed I said I am going to show you the secret. I didn't say I would tell it to you.

"You've all heard the secret for success many times—and for some of you, hearing it has made a tremendous difference in your lives—but for most of us, just hearing about something isn't enough.

"Many of you have read about the secret for success, as well. And although some of you have gained much from what you've read, the information alone was not enough to make a profound difference in the way you live and work.

"Do you remember, as a child, how you learned to walk . . . or ride a bicycle? You were shown. You watched grown-ups walking. You saw how they did it. Then, someone walked with you, helped you, picked you up when you fell, all the while holding your hands, and sooner or later you boldly stepped out, moved your legs and you walked.

"You were free at last!

"Someone put you on a bike and ran along beside you, holding the seat to keep it steady so you wouldn't fall off—and showed you how to do it. And one day—perhaps minutes after you were first shown how . . . maybe hours or even days—you rode that bicycle. It wobbled. You were afraid, but finally you took off down the sidewalk, riding the bike all by yourself.

"You were free at last!

"In each instance, although you knew much about how to walk and ride, that knowledge alone wasn't enough. You knew all about how, but you couldn't do it—yet. Knowing that information wasn't enough. In fact, what you knew was actually of little use to you.

"Looking back on it all, you might assume that what you thought you didn't know was the secret. That once you got that knowledge, once you learned that one thing you knew you didn't know yet, then you walked . . . then you rode your bike.

"But if you think back very carefully, you'll discover that the secret to walking, and the secret to riding, did not come from what you knew—and it did not come from what you thought you didn't know, either. That special secret lived somewhere in a vast expanse of unexplored knowledge—what I've learned to call 'what you don't know that you don't know.'

"Am I confusing you? I hope not. It's really a very simple idea, but it's the most powerful source of creativity and energy for accomplishment any of us can tap into.

"What walking and riding a bicycle are all about is balance. Balance is not something you have—like a possession. It's not something you do—such as moving this way or that—although both are required to some extent to achieve balance.

"Balance is a state of being. You either are in that state—or you are not. You are either walking—or falling down; riding—or crashing. Balance is the key.

"Once you attain the state of being balanced, you've got the secret. No one will ever take it away from you. It cannot be lost or stolen. It cannot even be forgotten—although you may experience moments when you don't remember that you remember, but they don't last long.

"Why am I telling you all of this? Some of you are asking yourselves that very question!" And his booming laugh filled the room as he said, "I can see by some faces that you are. Good!

"I'm telling you this about being shown, about what you don't know that you don't know, about balance, because success, having success and doing successful things, is exactly like acquiring balance. It is a state of being.

"You are either being successful—or you are not. There is no in between. It's a passing or failing grade. Black or white—no gray—like being pregnant.

"So, are you successful? Yes or no?

"Are you?"

He paused and again seemed to look at every one of us. For my part, I asked myself the question: yes or no, was I successful? I answered immediately—and out loud, "Yes."

He looked directly at me.

"You answered 'Yes'?" he asked, moving from the podium over to the side of the stage closest to me.

"Will you stand up, please?" he requested.

I did.

"You are successful," he said. "That's wonderful! Tell me, when did you realize that?"

"Sunday," I said.

"This past Sunday?"

"Yes," I laughed. "Just this past Sunday." I could hear the chuckles behind me throughout the audience.

"Please, come up on stage and tell us what happened," he asked.

I took a deep breath and looked at him. He smiled and encouraged me to join him on stage. I went up and stood next to him.

He introduced me to the audience, asked for a microphone for me, and as the man with the mike wired me for sound, he explained how we met.

He told the people about the man he first saw one short week ago, sitting in his hiding place in the back of the room. He reported in specific detail how I had described my business to him, how I had felt about that then, and what I was planning to do—that just this past Thursday I'd been at my "last meeting": I was quitting the business.

He told them about the success I had achieved—sponsoring new people, having my guests present tonight. He described my guests, how they seemed to him excited and enthusiastic about being here . . . how when he spoke with them, they had told him that discovering Network Marketing, finding a place and people who honored their values, that gave them a way to fulfill their life's purpose, was something for which they'd each been searching for years.

He told the audience about my life's purpose as I had shared it with him, the things I valued and what they meant to me, and what they provided for me.

As he spoke, I was touched by the pride that was evident in the way he talked about me. Literally, tears welled up in my eyes and I found myself raising my glasses to wipe my eyes clear. No one had ever said these things about me before. And certainly, no one had ever done so in front of a few hundred people.

He said, I was ". . . an inspiration for him."

He said, he was ". . . so proud of me."

He called me ". . . a young Master."

Then he said, "I promised that I would show you the secret for success. . . ."

He put one arm around my shoulders, pointed to me with the other hand, and said, "Here it is."

The silence of the room was a roar in my ears, the faces staring up at me a blur. I had the sensation of falling, yet I knew I was standing . . . floating, yet I knew my feet were firmly planted on the carpeted stage.

An image swept into my mind. It was crystal clear, sharp-edged, and vividly bright. It was a room filled with people, seen from the stage. I was the one in front looking out at them. They were standing, applauding, cheering. I had given them something that made a difference to them . . . something that moved and touched them . . . something that empowered them . . . inspired them, and they were acknowledging me. They came up to me on stage. They were shaking my hand. Thanking me. Telling me how much what I had said and done had meant to them.

One woman in particular stood out. She had hold of my hand in both of hers, and she was saying, "Thank you, thank you so much for showing me my life's purpose . . . for showing me how to believe . . . in myself."

I was snapped out of my movie by The Greatest Networker's arm, still around my shoulders, giving a firm squeeze and then letting go. He stood back and looked into my face and eyes. "You are very special to us," he said. "Now, show them success." And he walked off the stage.

In an instant, the people were on their feet applauding. There were cheers and people were shouting my name. I was in shock. I remember spreading my arms slightly and thanking them, smiling and saying, "Thank you, thank you so much."

As I looked over the standing crowd, the room filled with their enthusiastic applause, I saw him at the back of the room beside the door. Our eyes met. He smiled. And above all the cheers and clapping I heard his booming laugh. He raised his hand, waved to me, and walked out the door.

Amazing!

* * *

AMAZING indeed.

Ever since The Greatest Networker was first published, people have asked me if there would be another book, a sequel, perhaps even a series. I always asked in return, "If there was another book, what would it be about?"

The answer was nearly universal: "Tell us how he did it— how he built his business. Pick it up from where you left off and tell us the story of how he became such a success."

Okay. I will.

And I can tell you the "how," right now, in just one word—well, two really:

A Conversation

I KNOW, I KNOW. Way too simple, but that's how—a conversation.

Everything happens in conversation. Network Marketing is a conversation. Life's a conversation. I changed my habits of belief with a conversation—actually a number of them. That's how I learned everything I know—and don't know, and don't know that I don't know—about everything.

And it happened with lightening speed.

All right, I'm getting ahead of both of us.

After that meeting Thursday night a thousand years ago, after I'd walked my guests to the door, I went over to my car. The gray truck was gone. Chris, the doorman, was still there, and as he opened my door for me and I slid in to my seat, he handed me a note.

"This was on your windshield," he said. "Have a great night."

"Thanks, Chris," I said as I opened the note. It read:

Up for a little late dinner?
Japanese this time?
Hiroshi's—it's on 9th Street.
See you there.

* * *

ALTHOUGH I DIDN'T know it at the time, that night was the beginning of my "formal" and ever-so-brief training in, and on, how to build a successful Network Marketing business. My training sessions were all conversations—conversations with my mentor. To this day, I train my people the very same way.

CHAPTER ONE

A New Definition
of Belief

T HE ENTRANCE TO the restaurant was on the street
level and opened onto a tall, narrow, wood-paneled
staircase leading to the second floor. As I reached
the top of the stairs, I heard gentle harp-like music interrupted by The Greatest Networker's familiar booming laugh
coming from inside. The doorway that opened into Hiroshi's
was covered by a blue and white cloth banner that hung
down in two separate pieces. I had to part and walk through
them to go inside.

The restaurant was small and immediately felt warm and
friendly. Off to the right, there were six chairs in front of
what I learned was the sushi bar, but there were no other
chairs in sight. All the low tables—there were eight or nine
of them—were arranged on straw mats raised off the ground
on platforms about one and a half feet from the wooden
floor. Each table was surrounded by flat, square cushions in

the same blue and white designs as the cloth "door" I'd just come through.

My friend was seated cross-legged at the farthest table. As I approached him I was greeted by a chorus of Japanese voices—from a bowing waitress in a kimono, the smiling man behind the sushi bar who wore a blue sash as a head-band, and other invisible greetings coming from a number of hidden somewheres.

"What did they say?" I asked, as I stood next to his table.

"*Konbanwa*," he told me. "It means 'Good evening,' and Hiroshi also asked how you were. So, how *are* you?"

As I began to answer him, he motioned for me to sit and instructed me to take off my shoes. I noticed his were placed neatly under the edge of the raised wooden, mat-covered platform he was sitting on. I took my shoes off and placed them next to his and slid across from him at the table.

"Here," he said, and bent down to look under the low table urging me to do the same. "See, there's a place for you to put your legs."

As he sat up again he continued, "It's usually pretty un-comfortable for Westerners to sit with their legs crossed the whole time it takes to enjoy a Japanese meal. But Hiroshi is very accommodating, so he's cut out these spaces under the tables for us gaijin to stretch out our legs, bend our knees, and sit comfortably like we were in a chair. Traditional Japanese people would rather sit perched on these small fu-tons," he said, pointing to one of the thin cushions we were both seated on.

"So, how are you? Quite a week—yes?"

"I'll say. Gosh, I'm really, really *great*, thank you. How are you?"

"Proud and pleased with you for one thing." He smiled his biggest, broadest grin.

"There's that smile I want to package and sell," I laughed, pointing to his beaming face.

"Ah yes, *that* smile," he said, clearly pleased. "Want to know a secret?" he asked, leaning towards me with an expectant expression.

"Sure," I said.

"This smile was something I taught myself to do. In fact, I first used it to change my thoughts and attitude."

"How so?"

"Well, I once heard a Networker talk to a group of people he was training. He was speaking to them about negativity, how many of the skeptical thoughts and pessimistic attitudes in this business stem from rejection. He explained how he used a smile to change his attitude.

"Now, I am by nature a worrier. You look surprised! It's true," he told me. "I can worry about anything and everything, mostly the future. At least I used to—and I still do to some extent. You know that—what's the word . . . acronym? F.E.A.R: False Expectations Appearing Real. I'm a master of that.

"Anyway, this guy who was training asked the audience to do an experiment with him. He told them that in a moment he was going to have them think a negative thought. Anything *bad* would do, he told us. Then, once we had that pessimistic thought in place, he said he was going to have us do something really interesting and just see what happened.

3

"So, we all got our angry or afraid or critical or worrying thoughts in place. He told us to put our hands up, then lower them when we had our unhappy thought firmly in our minds. As soon as all our hands were down, he shouted, 'Now, *smile!* It doesn't matter if you're still worried or angry—just *smile!* Big. Huge. Ear-to-ear grins. Come on!' he yelled. '*Smile!*'

"Well, most everyone in the audience broke up laughing. Then he asked us, 'What happened?'

"Seems no one in the group could maintain their negative thoughts with smiles on their faces. He explained it was impossible to stay angry or worried while you were smiling. In fact, he told us that the mind is incapable of holding a negative and positive thought at the same time. He said science had discovered that when you smile, the brain releases a flood of endorphin-like chemicals along with a series of signals much like electricity that make having and holding negative thoughts physiologically impossible. It was fascinating. *Fascinating!*"

"Amazing," I thought out loud.

"Let me ask you something. I know that in the past—not this last week," he smiled again for emphasis, cocking his head like a poodle who just heard a strange sound it didn't understand, "but in the past, you've had some times when your thinking was pretty pessimistic—true?"

"Oh yeah," I said with surprising conviction from an immediate recall of too many negative feelings.

"What did you do then to change your mind?"

"Well, mostly I didn't—change my mind, I mean."

"You weren't negative *all the time*, were you?" he asked, leaning forward and looking directly at me in that earnest,

4

genuinely concerned manner of his that heard everything and accepted it as true.

"No, of course not," I replied, noticing my answer was simply matter-of-fact and not defensive as had so often been the case. "I'd just wait until it passed. I mean, eventually I would forget what I was worrying about—at least for a time. Until I started feeling angry, upset, or scared again," I added.

"Good. So now you know all you have to do is smile. What do they say, '*Smile* is the biggest word in our language, because there's a *mile* to go before the end of it'? Whenever you're thinking negative thoughts, just plaster a big grin on your face and watch what happens. You know what I started doing after I first learned that smile exercise?"

I nodded for him to tell me.

"I put a mirror right next to my telephone. Then, every time I made a prospecting or follow-up call, I'd check my reflection and make sure I was smiling. The results were astounding! I can't tell you how much easier my calls became—*and* how much more successful. It happened quickly, too. That smile thing really works fast."

* * *

AS IF FROM out of nowhere, food began to arrive—plate after plate after plate of it! Each one small, a different shape and size and color: china, bamboo, little wooden platforms. And on almost every one was something I'd never seen the likes of before.

"Wow! What's all of this?" I exclaimed, waving my hand over the array of exotic dishes in front of us.

Pointing to each one in turn, The Greatest Networker told me their Japanese names and what they meant in English. Colorful red, yellow, and white vegetable pickles that he said I'd find a tad salty. A salad made of seaweed. (He laughed at the expression on my face when he said "seaweed.") Pieces of broiled chicken on skewers. Broiled eel, too. (Another reaction. Another laugh from him.) Oshitashi—a fancy name for spinach, he told me with a smile. Tofu. (I reacted. He didn't.) Tempura—deep-fried carrots, squash, mushrooms, onions, broccoli, and shrimp. A bamboo plate of green noodles with a small cup of dark sauce for dipping them. A selection of raw fish he explained was sushi without the rice, including oysters and snails with tiny hand-carved toothpicks to eat them with.

I'd eaten in one of those Japanese steak houses before, where the chef is part entertainer, chopping and juggling while cooking your food on a grill right in front of you at your table, but this was something altogether different.

"I thought you might enjoy sampling a variety of dishes," he told me, gesturing for me to begin.

It was my first time using chopsticks, and I immediately asked for pointers.

He patiently showed me how to hold them, one cradled between my thumb and forefinger, the other resting against the remaining fingers of my right hand. It was fun—and I was *awful* at it.

"Just think of them as two extra long fingers," he laughed, effortlessly scooping up a piece of raw fish and dipping it into a little round dish full of dark, brown sauce.

"Tamari," he answered my silent question. "It's a special kind of soy sauce."

He closed his eyes savoring the morsel in his mouth, slowly and deliberately chewing with great relish. "Oh, that is so good! Hamachi, yellow tail. Here, try some," he said and gestured to some light beige slices of fresh fish arranged on the plate in the shape of a fan.

I reached for the fish. Got one. Promptly dropped it on the table. Got it again and placed it triumphantly in the little dish of soy sauce he'd poured for me.

He showed me how to hold one of the small bowls of rice in my left hand as a portable dish and serve myself any of the items in front of us by resting it on the rice, explaining it was quite proper and might help until my expertise with my two new wooden "fingers" increased.

The food was truly wonderful. I don't think I'd ever experienced so many new and honestly delicious flavors at one time before and told him so. He was clearly pleased.

"So tell me," he asked, "what made the difference for you this week?"

I sat up straight and unfolded my legs from their crossed position to place them in the space beneath the table, which really felt great, because they'd begun to stiffen up quite a bit.

"I believe! I believe!" I said in a voice mimicking someone at a Sunday tent revival.

"Good," he laughed. "What is it that you believe?"

"Me," I answered instantly. "I believe in me. I believe I can do this business. I believe in my success . . . my ability to learn . . . my goals . . . my future. . . ."

"That's great," he said. "Tell me, what do you mean when you use the word *belief?*"

"Hmmm," I thought out loud. "That's a good question."

"Thank you," he said smartly. "I love asking good questions."

"Well, what I mean is that I *know*," I answered. "Like with my goals, I *trust* that what I'm thinking about will come true. It's kind of like—no, it's exactly like having *faith*."

"My turn," he said. "Hmmm. That's a good answer."

"Thank you," I quipped. "I love having good answers."

"Bright boy. Charming boy," he smiled, "and learns so quickly, too. Seriously, though, I've been thinking about this a lot recently—this business of belief. I know it's at the source of success. Belief is the essence of creativity. It's imperative for us to *believe*.

"Clearly *lack* of belief—in themselves, their products, the company, the industry, their abilities—is a big stumbling block that stops so many people in our business. As it was for you, yes?"

"Yes," I answered.

"Now, you said that for you, belief was *knowing*. Is that right?"

"Yes, like having faith. I *know* this or that is so, and because I know it will come true I can do it."

"Great," he said, obviously warming to the conversation. He leaned forward, setting down his chopsticks, and bored into my face with that intense gaze of his. "Okay, *how do you know?*"

"What do you mean *how? I know*, that's all." I could feel a hint of defensiveness come out through my voice.

He put his hand up, gently, in a gesture that clearly meant "stop."

"Look, stay with me on this. Help me take a look at this, 'cause I'm really fascinated by the notion of belief and I think I may be on to something really important. Will you do a little exercise with me?"

"Okay," I volunteered.

"I warn you, this could get a little rough for you for a moment or two. It is what someone once described to me as the most uncomfortable exercise he'd ever done. If I guess right, we're going to have your defenses up real quick. But don't worry. It won't last longer than a minute or two—max."

That *charming* introduction really had me afraid of doing the exercise—and already plugged-in—and I told him so.

He simply smiled that knowing smile of his and raised his eyebrows in invitation.

"Okay," I exhaled and began to sing, "Too late to turn back now . . . I believe. I believe. I believe I'm falling . . ." and let the song trail off. "Let's get it over with."

"Cool," he exclaimed with excitement, rubbing his hands together. "So tell me a fact—something you absolutely *know*."

"The world is round," I said convincingly.

"Great!" he almost shouted. "How do you *know* that?"

"I've seen the pictures of the Earth the astronauts took from space."

"And how do you know *that*?"

"What, that I've seen the pictures? Or that it was really Earth . . . or really a photograph. . . . What?"

"Please," he said, with a beseeching quality in his voice, "try not to become *too* clever here." He smiled at me. "Just look at the question and tell me: How do you know that?"

I was only on my third answer to his questions and already my uneasiness was all too clear and much too present—and my expectation was that this discomfort was only going to get worse. In my mind, I was already racing ahead in the conversation, wanting to get the exercise over with as fast as possible.

How did I know?

I saw the pictures, the photographs.

How did I know *that?*

I'd seen them with my own two eyes.

How did I know *that?*

I'd *seen* them, that's how. Looked right at them right in front of me right in the pages of some magazine or on TV. *That's how!*

And how did I know *that?*

The picture of the Earth enters the eyes and is focused on the retina as tiny bits of light upside down. The brain sets it right-side up again, and the electrical impulses of the pixel pieces of the photo travel through the neurotransmitters and synapses of the cerebral cortex and . . . Man, I have no idea *how* I know. *I just know.* The Earth is round. I *know!* That's all!

"I can see you reached the most uncomfortable part of the exercise already," he said softly, his face expressionless.

"Let me guess—you're now at the point of insisting that you *know,* and yet not being able to say why. Just, '*I know!* And let's quit fooling around.' Right?"

He didn't wait for me to answer. "Or, perhaps you're over at the opposite side, realizing that you absolutely *don't know*. Which is it—or is it both?"

I sighed, long and slow. I'd been here before with him. Impossible questions. Baffling thoughts.

"I guess I don't *know*. I don't *know* anything! I don't know that I don't know!" I blurted out, my frustration obvious to us both.

We sat in silence for a time. His gaze never left my face. His expression revealed nothing.

Finally, he said, "*Ri-ight*," drawing the word out long and slow as if to make it its own complete sentence.

"I sympathize, my friend. I, too, found the exercise most uncomfortable. After I did it, I had the thought that I simply didn't know *anything*," As he said this, The Greatest Networker shook his head and seemed truly saddened by the remembrance. "And that didn't sit well with me. I am—or was—the kind of person who really *needed to know*, and to *be right*, too."

He looked away as he often did when he was recalling something and said almost to himself, "Do you mean to say all I ever thought I knew, I really didn't? I just made it all up? And all anybody else knew, that was all made up as well? Whew! Boggles the mind. . . . Absolutely.

"*Bu-ut*," he said and then paused to take a deep breath, "let's keep it simple for the moment. Given our at best—confused relationship to *knowing*, where does that leave us with *believing*?"

"I can see the thought puzzles you, too," he said, smiling his agreement with me. "Your definition of belief had a lot

11

to do with knowing what you believed was right and true—yes?"

I nodded that it did.

"So did mine. Once. But I've got another meaning for the word now, and I'm certain that I'm really on to something. Given the very real possibility that we make all of this stuff up anyway," he said, his hand sweeping wide across the table, "I think I'll stick with this new thought of mine for a while. It's far more empowering. Here's what I'm thinking about. . . ."

* * *

"THE WORD BELIEF is made up of two parts," he told me. "*Be* is the first part, and you and I have already talked a bunch about being—yes? In order to *have* success and *do* successful things, you have to be *being* successful—right?"

Two questions, two nods from me in the affirmative.

"Great. Now here's the fun and insightful bit. The second part of *belief* is *lief*, which comes from the Indo-European *leubh*, which means . . ." and he paused dramatically, punctuating the moment with his hands spread open and apart, palms up, " . . . *love*."

As he said that, he raised his knees up under his chin, wrapping his arms around them and looking at me with an almost impish twinkle, asking, "And what do you think of that, my young friend?"

"Be . . . love. You're saying to believe means to *be love*?"

"What if it did?" he asked quickly in return. "What if instead of having to know for a fact in order to believe in something, all you had to do was love it?"

12

That was indeed an idea I wanted to think about. What if when I believed, I simply loved the notion? What if. . . .

"Talk to me," he said, pulling me out of my thoughts. "Life is a conversation. As Plato said, 'The truth is revealed in dialogue.' Talking to yourself like there's somebody there to talk to won't cut it. Talk to *me*. Tell *me* what you just thought you were thinking?"

"Okay," I said, shaking my head at his odd, yet welcome, tenacity.

"I was thinking about how when we first met, you asked me about my goals. At the time, I remember *thinking*. . . ." and I stressed the word and looked across the table at him with a raised eyebrow to show I used the statement advisedly.

He smiled. I continued.

"I remember thinking that there was no use in having goals, because I didn't believe I could ever achieve them."

"*Bingo!*" he exclaimed nearly jumping forward. "So, what do you suppose the constant message you were giving your subconscious mind was with *that* thought?"

"Not good."

"Imagine for a moment," he asked thoughtfully, "how many people in the world don't make goals, don't have a vision, have stopped dreaming, all because they just don't *believe* it's true—in the conventional sense of the word—that it, whatever *it* is, will ever work out for them?

"You know," he continued, "a Harvard research project years ago revealed that only 3 percent of the U.S. adult population had written goals. Do you suppose the other 97 percent would be more interested in writing down their dreams for the future if they knew they didn't have to have unshakable *belief* that they could and would achieve them? They just had to be *in love* with them—they just had to fall *in love* with their goals and dreams?"

"Wow," I thought and said—then said again. "*Wow.*"

"As I said," he confided, "I really think I'm on to something here."

I couldn't help myself. I became lost in a swirl of thoughts. I began talking to myself about *be loving* my goals—as if there was somebody there to talk to.

Amazing.

* * *

WE LEFT HIROSHI'S 'round midnight. I was as full of wonderful food as I was of wonder about our conversation. As we walked to our cars—my car, his familiar gray pick-up truck—he asked, "So how can I help you?" and looked over at me with an expectant expression.

My immediate response was thinking I didn't need any help—well, not true, not at all. I just didn't feel comfortable with what I really wanted to ask for. I was afraid of what he'd think about me for asking.

Yeah, I was fearful of the rejection—*his* rejection of *me*. But instead of my usual gosh 'n' golly ashamed silence, I mustered the courage to tell him what I'd just been thinking.

He listened intently, staring directly into my eyes. When I'd finished explaining what was going on with me, ending by acknowledging the "False Expectations Appearing . . ." thing, he smiled and said, "You are quite the quick study, my friend. Thank you for telling me the thoughts you had. I appreciate your honesty. I appreciate you."

It amazed me how good he could make me feel and how quickly.

"So what is it you really want to ask for?"

It amazed me how uncomfortable he could make me feel how quickly, as well.

I took a deep breath and simply decided to ask flat-out: "I want you to be my mentor." I immediately felt a weird combination of relief *and* apprehension.

"Love to," he said instantly.

"*R-really?*" I asked and answered, stammering my surprise.

"No, I lied," he said, and let out such a laugh from way deep down I was afraid he'd wake the entire neighborhood.

"*R-r-really*," he mimicked, "I'd love to. It would be an honor. And what is it that you want me to be your mentor for?"

"I want to learn how to build my business. I want to be as successful as you are in Network Marketing." I told him. "I want . . . I want to. . . ."

"Ye-es," he encouraged, playfully.

"I want to be The Greatest Networker in the World," I said, certain I'd said it in a way that added an unspoken "Is that okay for me to say?" to the end of my sentence.

As if reading my mind, he answered, "That's okay. I wouldn't have it any other way. Every true teacher's goal is to have his students surpass him. And that's especially true in Network Marketing. A sponsor who isn't committed to his people being more successful than he is isn't a sponsor. He's an impostor. . . . An *impostor*," he repeated, obviously pleased with what he'd just said.

"Do you know where 'mentor' comes from?" he asked, holding open my car door for me as I got in.

"No clue," I told him. "No, wait!" I exclaimed remembering a shadow of something from college. "The Odyssey. Odysseus—Ulysses. Mentor was some kind of king or something."

"Close. Mentor was Odysseus's counselor, his trusted friend. He stayed behind, instead of going off to the Trojan War, to protect Odysseus's home and family. We owe Homer and the Greeks for the idea of having a mentor/advisor. Another meaning of the word relates to the root word *men*, as in *mental*—to think. Interesting—yes?"

"Interesting yes. Does that mean, as my mentor, you make me think?"

"To the extent I can *make* you do anything, I suppose it does. One request, though," he added.

"Let's agree to do our thinking out loud. I am devoted to the idea—I have a 'devotion to the notion'—that our entire lives are conversations."

"Can you say more about that?"

"I will. It's late, though, and I'm guessing you need to get home."

"True," I told him.

"Just one more thing before you go," he said, closing my car door and leaning down to speak to me through the open window.

"There is really only one subject worth having a mentor for—at least, there is only one area in which I'm interested and committed to being your mentor."

16

"Yes?"

"Living your Life Purpose. Everything else comes out of that. Your dreams and goals, your vision, your values, the mission of your business, are all anchored in your Life Purpose. When you're faced with a challenge, your Purpose will guide you through. When opportunities present themselves, you'll choose the best avenue to pursue based on its fit with your Life Purpose. It is, as they say, what gets you out of bed in the morning. It's what you will use to measure your progress. It's the track you run on, and the place to go back to when you get off track."

"I understand," I said thoughtfully.

"And as I remember," he reflected, "your Life Purpose is to be a teacher—a teacher committed to people living their own Life Purposes. Yes?"

"Absolutely," I said, a bit amazed and nonetheless pleased he remembered.

"So," he mused, "what you're asking is that I be the mentor of a mentor—is that correct?"

"I guess it is," I agreed.

"Far out! I love it!" he exclaimed with obvious pleasure, walked over to his truck, jumped up and in and drove away.

Chapter Two
If You Knew
What I Know. . . .

D URING A TELEPHONE CALL the next day, I
agreed to meet The Greatest Networker that Saturday morning and drive with him to a training he
was presenting in another city, about an hour or so away
from my home. He said he'd pick me up outside my apart-
ment at 8:00 so we could arrive by 9:00. The training itself
started at 10:00.

I'd been standing outside since a quarter to eight, listening to the sounds of the city waking up, wishing I could live
somewhere where nature spoke louder than construction
equipment and garbage trucks, when I heard his big voice
shout, "Good morning!"

I looked around expecting to see his gray truck, so I
was surprised to see him leaning out of a gleaming black
Mercedes—the kind with the big round bug-eye head-
lights—pulling up to the curb across the street.

"Morning," I greeted him as he gestured for me to climb in beside him. "I didn't notice you. I was watching for the truck."

"Not today."

"This is quite a car," I said appreciatively.

"Yes, it is," he agreed. "Best I've ever owned. It's a luxury tank. Darn near drives itself."

"What model is it?" I asked.

"It's an E320. I'd rather have a 420," he said as we pulled away quickly—*very* quickly—from the curb. "This is a six cylinder and that one's an eight. But this has constant four-wheel drive, and I want that for winter. The 420s don't come with it—yet. I would like the extra juice of that fat V-8, though. I think that's what I like best about my truck."

"This seems plenty fast,' I commented, and he nodded agreement.

"Is this an 'S' Class?" I asked, remembering reading somewhere that a number of experts considered the S-Class Mercedes to be the finest car in the world. Isn't that what The Greatest Networker should and would drive, I thought. Then I remembered his beloved pick-up truck.

"Nope. Just a plain ol' E-Class," he answered with a grin. "Those 'S' cars are crazy expensive. I could get this plus a BMW motorcycle for a spare tire with what just *one* of them costs. Besides, I just don't like the way they look—too much extra body stuff. I like this just fine—except," he paused, "I *hate* the color!"

"Why. It looks great," I said.

"Black is such a *mess* to keep clean," he explained, and with an unusual amount of passion at that. "It shows every speck of dust and dirt, and don't even think about bugs and birds! If anyone even walks near it, it scratches and I'm really just too much of a perfectionist for scratches. I should have gotten the silver color I wanted, but I let Rebecca talk me into this." Rebecca was his daughter.

"How so?" I asked.

"It was an ego mistake on my part. She said black was sexy. She said silver was an 'old man's color.' I told her I *was* old. Heck, I even drive at the speed limit all the time now. I'm convinced most other drivers are nuts. They don't have a clue they're aiming multi-ton weapons down the road at 60 miles per hour while dialing their cell phones and reaching for a fist-full of Micky D's fries. And, I don't particularly care to drive at night much anymore either.

"Now that, my friend," he said turning to me, "is *old!*" And we both laughed.

"Silver," he said, almost to himself. "The next one will be silver. Bad news is," he added, "I'll have to live with black for five years, maybe more. These cars are designed and built so well they last *too* long."

"So listen . . ." I said, after a brief silence.

"I do make the attempt," he replied with a smile.

"I know you do," I laughed. "Better than anyone I know." I continued, "I'm curious why you're going to speak today to a group from a competing Networking company. You don't see a conflict in that?"

"Sure, I *see* a conflict," he admitted. "I just don't *care* about the conflict. It's not important to me. Do you know those wonderful ads for that Kosher hot dog company— what's the name?"

"The ones that picture a Rabbi saying, 'We answer to a higher authority,'" I replied.

"The very same. That's what it's like for me. I know many companies and many Networking leaders in the industry are of the opinion that nothing ever goes cross-line, much less cross-company. I just don't happen to agree."

"What about maintaining the integrity of the system a group is using?" I asked. "I've read articles in *Upline* and a number of books that say you should never do that. 'The system is the solution,' they say. Don't mess with it, because anything else is not duplicatable."

"My, you are a well-read and knowledgeable young man, especially for one who was about to quit the business for lack of success—when was that, a week, ten days ago?"

He glanced over at me with a good-natured grin, and I laughed and shook my head.

"Gotcha," he joked. "Couldn't resist. Seriously, your point is well taken. So let me explain both about what I'm up to and this whole business of systems. First, this systems thing.

"I never teach others quote *business-building how to* un-quote. That's between a direct upline sponsor and his or her people. What works successfully for one product and one compensation plan often and usually will not work for others. I never want to conflict with a given company's culture—or the culture of a given distributor downline. They are too hard to create and keep going and growing for me to fool with—even intelligently.

"I maintain all the *how to* you ever need to know to do this business successfully can be learned in a single hour or one short afternoon. I never spend more than an hour or an hour and a half on the 'how to' with my people," he told me.

"It's the *why to* and the *who to* that interest me most. Those are universal. I don't care if your product is long distance phone service, pills, potions, lotions, or Web sites. It doesn't matter if your comp plan is a breakaway, unilevel, binary, or urinary. . . ."

I couldn't help but laugh at that last one—as I'm sure he intended.

"What I train about is *who to be* to be successful in this business," he continued. "That's what's really important to me and I say to you, too. That's what everybody *really* needs to know—and so very few people *really* do.

"This business is relationship-*led.* . . ."

He looked over at me to see if I understood and must have noticed something lacking in my expression, for he continued, "I see. Okay. You've read phrases in business books like, 'profit *driven*' or 'product *driven*'—yes?"

I replied that I had and quoted a line Benjamin Franklin once said: "Drive thy business, or it will drive thee."

"Great!" he exclaimed, "Ben Franklin said that? Far out. Well, what if ol' Ben had said instead, '*Lead* thy business, or thy business will *lead* thee'?"

When I didn't answer, he said, "Let me tell you a story that beautifully explains the difference between being *driven* and being *led.* Have you ever heard of a man named Joe Batten?"

I told him I hadn't.

"Mr. Batten is one of the grand old men of public speaking. He's a member of the National Speakers Association

Hall of Fame and he wrote the business bestseller *Tough-minded Leadership*.

"Some years ago, Joe was meeting with a group of 35 corporate CEOs for a day-long seminar. Early in the presentation, he asked, 'How many of you are leaders in your company?' Of course, every person in the room raised a hand.

"Joe smiled and said, 'I'll ask you the same question *after* I share this true story with you.'

"'In the Middle East,' Joe told them, 'there are two countries separated by a common border, both of which have large wool and mutton industries. The cultures of the two countries are radically different and hostile to each other. In fact, they have fought wars with each other and are fighting as we speak.'

"'In one country, the shepherds walk behind their flocks.

"'In the other country, the shepherds walk in front of their flocks.

"'Now remember,' Joe told them, 'this is a *true story*.'

"Joe continued: 'In the country where the shepherds walk behind their flocks, the quality of the mutton and the wool is poor and it is not a profitable industry. In the country where the shepherds walk in front of their flocks, the quality of the mutton and wool is excellent and the profitability is high.'

"Then Joe asked the group, '*Why?*' Nobody answered, so Joe told them.

"'In the flocks where the shepherd walks behind and drives, pushes, corrects, and is always in charge, the young sheep grow up afraid to stray from the flock for fear of being rapped up-side the head by the shepherd's staff or having the dogs sent out to round them up. They have no opportunity to explore for better grass and water, or to play with other young lambs. They simply become obedient, passive, and apathetic. By the time they are grown, they have lost all initiative. They are not really healthy. They are *driven*.

"'In the country where the shepherds walk in front of their flocks,' Joe continued on, 'the young lambs have plenty of opportunity to stray, play, experiment, and then catch up to the flock. Instead of feeling controlled, compressed, repressed, depressed, and suppressed, they feel free, empowered, enhanced, and stretched. They eat more, sleep better, and grow up large and healthy. They are *led*.'

"Now, when Joe finished his story," The Greatest Networker said, "assuring the assembled executives again of its authenticity, he asked them once more, 'How many of you truly *lead* in your company?'"

The Greatest Networker turned and looked at me, asking, "Would it surprise you to learn not a hand was raised?"

* * *

"AS I SAID," he went on, "we are a relationship-*led* industry. And while I'm at it, who does the *leading* in Network Marketing—the companies or the distributor representatives?"

"The company, of course," I answered.

He made the sound of a buzzer, like the ones on old TV quiz shows, and said, "*Wrong!* Oh, you're right in terms of how it *is* today, for the most part. But I don't think that's how it was designed. And it's certainly *not* how it *has* to be. That's not Network Marketing's natural structure. This business is distributor *led*. No distributors—no Network organizations—no sales. No sales—no company.

"My friend, you and I are independent contractors, Network Marketing professionals. The companies are, in fact, wholesale suppliers. They're our *vendors*. We buy their goods and services and re-sell them to the consumers, or we sell them *for them* making a commission on sales made by ourselves and our Network organizations. We market the company's products by contractual agreement—remember the 'Distributor Agreement' you signed?"

I did, and said so.

"I remember mine. It made it clear I was not their employee. I am the CEO of a free enterprise wholly owned by me. It's not their company. *It's mine*," he said with conviction.

He sat back deeply in his seat. "Whoa," he said with a deep exhale, "I got going on that one. Well, it is something I'm really passionate about. For years I've heard corporate Networking executives say they can't allow the tail to wag the dog. Well, who's the dog and who's the tail?"

"I got it," I told him, a little taken aback by his intensity.

As if sensing my apprehension, he laughed and apologized, "I'm sorry. This one always gets me going. I've got half a mind to start a worldwide distributor association. I think we need one desperately. Can you imagine if even just a small percentage of the 20 million or so of us involved in Network Marketing in North America all got on the same one or two pages together? Wow! There's nothing we couldn't do.

"Do you know what just one million people who really knew how to talk to people—you know: tell five who tell

five, or two who tell two—do you have any idea what that
many people with those communication and persuasion
skills could accomplish in the next presidential election?
Boggles the mind. 'Rich DeVos for president!'" he added,
and he laughed his booming laugh.

He was right, of course. It certainly boggled my mind.

And beyond our obvious political clout, I thought to myself, what if a whole bunch of successful Network Marketers
came together to share what they've learned about this business with each other—and share *that* with those who weren't
so successful yet? I imagined the scene of distributor leaders
in this industry meeting at some marvelous resort hotel to
discuss what works and what doesn't, to explore new ideas
and discover together better ways of doing things.

What a picture. "What if . . ." indeed.

It would be like Napoleon Hill's Mastermind, although
on a scale larger by far than even the farsighted author of
Think and Grow Rich would have imagined.

This one, I thought, would continue to "boggle my mind"
for some time.

* * *

"ALL RIGHT," he said with another deep breath, bringing
me back from my Mastermind dream, "where were we? Ah
yes, *relationships*. This business is led by relationships.

"Relationships are where the rubber meets the road in
Network Marketing—the top *and* bottom line. That's the
train I'm on and what I train on: How to get into a relationship with another human being quickly and deeply at the

level of values, dealing with what's really important to people.

"You know, if all you did was get into one relationship with someone new each week, for 50 weeks, taking two weeks off for good and productive behavior," he laughed, "at the end of a year, or two at the most, you'd be sitting on top of a huge, successful Network Marketing organization. Tell me, you brought *how many* people to the meeting last Thursday?"

"Well, I brought three myself, and two of them brought one each themselves. That's five."

"Ever brought any guests before?" he asked.

I'd invited 20, probably more. A number of people promised to come, but no one ever showed up. "Nope. Not a soul," I admitted.

"Let's not get into religion," he quipped. "And how long have you been at this?"

"Four months," I groaned.

"And two of the people who came Thursday were already sponsored into the business by you—is that right?"

"Yes," I said. "That's correct."

"So what did you do differently this time?"

Honestly, I hadn't thought about it and told him so.

"So, think now," he instructed. "Tell me what you did."

"Well," I quickly started running movies of what had transpired with each of my guests and the two people I sponsored last week.

He interrupted my private 'screenings.' "Talk to me," he said.

"I'm looking at the movies of what I did when we met together," I told him.

"Great. Describe them to me."

"Well, I met two of them for lunch. We've had lunch together many times. We all three work together. My boss and I talked in his office."

"Great," he said again. "What was different about your talks with them this time? What happened?"

"Well," I said, recalling our lunches together and my meeting with my boss, "we have a favorite restaurant right next door to the office where we go for lunch most of the time. It's a deli, fast, convenient, clean—and *cheap*—and the food's pretty good. So I sat down with Emily first, and I just started talking to her."

"Who asked the most questions?" he wanted to know.

"Oh, I did. By far," I told him.

"Was that different for you—asking *her* questions?"

"Yes, I guess so."

"Was it or wasn't it?" he demanded patiently.

"Yes, it *was* different." Absolutely, I realized. "In fact, I don't think I've ever asked her that many questions before."

"Up for another story?" he asked.

I was and said so.

"A friend of mine named Richard told me this years ago," he said. "It's one of my favorites—a true story about a psychiatrist who was doing a research project for a book he was writing.

"The psychiatrist bought a first-class plane ticket from New York to L.A. The project was this: He would engage the person sitting next to him in a conversation where he, the psychiatrist, wouldn't make any statements at all, only ask his seatmate questions, during the entire six-hour flight—okay?"

I replied that I understood.

"So," he continued, "the plane lands in L.A., and the psychiatrist has his team of researchers interview his seat-mate. Now remember, the psychiatrist only asked this man questions.

"Two key points came out of the researcher's interview: First, the man who sat next to the psychiatrist *didn't know his name.* Pretty solid evidence that the psychiatrist indeed gave him no information at all, only asked questions.

"Point two," The Greatest Networker said, turning to-wards me for emphasis, "and this is the remarkable part—the man who sat next to the psychiatrist and answered question after question for six hours said the psychiatrist was *the single most interesting person he had ever met in his life!*"

Cool, I thought. "Wow! That's *amazing!*"

"Indeed," he agreed.

"You know, when you ask me questions about myself, you're talking about my favorite subject!" he said, and laughed his booming laugh.

"Is that true for you, too?" he asked me. "Aren't you the most *fascinating* person you know?"

"Well, I . . . I'd like to think. . . ."

"*Oh, come on,*" he interrupted, graciously saving me from more stammering. "I know, I know," he said, raising his hand to stop me. "You are such a modest and polite young man," he said, "that you find it quite the challenge to be honest about finding yourself *so* fascinating.

"Well, I'll take the responsibility for your thoughts—on this one. You *are* fascinating *to you.* We are all fascinating *to ourselves.* And we'd better be—don't you think? We spend more time with us than anyone else. We've known ourselves since we were very young—all our lives, in fact. We live together, work together, eat together, *sleep together. . . .*" We both laughed.

"Oh, yes," he said as he finished chuckling, nodding his head up and down, "when we really tell the truth, we find ourselves absolutely *fascinating*.

"Which is *why*," he continued immediately, "when you ask your prospects questions about who they are, how they are, what they love to do, what turns them off and on, and what they want for the future, they'll very likely find you to be the most interesting person they've ever met. They'll like you—right away. You're instantly in relationship and you've begun to make a friend.

"Why?" he asked and answered himself, "Because you're interested in their favorite subject. You're interested in them. And believe me, they will take it personally.

"Does this make sense to you?" he asked me after a moment.

"Sure," I told him. "Perfect sense."

"Look, what's really important here," he stressed, "is that for a Network Marketer, this business of asking people questions about who they are and what's really important to them—*and* listening creatively, openly, by design, to their answers—are the most fundamental of all skills. They are the keys to getting quickly and deeply into relationship with others. It's not simply *how* to be with them—it's *who* to be. Literally, you are *being* relationship. And, as I said earlier, that's really all you need do to succeed handsomely in this business.

"So tell me some of the things you found out about Emily as you were *being* a relationship with her."

"Well, she wants to go back to school." I told him. "She's convinced she can't get a better position at work unless she has a degree, and she wants very much to be a leader.

"She wants to put her daughter in private school, too. She lives in a neighborhood that's not all that great, and her daughter—Sara's her name—isn't doing all that well in public school, even though she's very bright. The other kids pick on her and she complains that her teachers don't really care. Ah, what else. . . ."

I told him all I could remember about my meeting with Emily, and Sandy, and Bob, my boss. He pressed me for details of each encounter and wanted to be clear about each point I described, especially *why* each person thought or felt the way they did about whichever topic of conversation I was describing.

He was especially interested in what my friends' *values* were, and kept asking me questions to clarify what I'd learned about them.

"Values. . . ." I played with the word and the thought. "Values are really important to you. I remember when we first met at your house, you kept asking me about my values. Why?"

"To begin with," he said, "all our relationships are based in, on, and around our values. When we share another person's values, we feel close to them immediately. Intimate. Strangers are people whose values we don't know about—yet.

"Sometimes we're attracted to people whose values are very different from ours. There's a great attraction between opposites, like yin and yang, man and woman. This is espe-

cially true when other people have values we'd like to cultivate for ourselves.

"For example, my dear friend Richard has the values of
play and having fun *big time*. By the way he's the one who
told me the story about the psychiatrist.

"If he could, Richard would spend the rest of his life playing: water skiing, snow skiing, jet skiing, golfing, bungee
jumping, speed boating, ballooning, sky diving, scuba diving.
. . . You name it, if it's *fun*, he'd be doing it.

"I'm more sedentary by nature, not all that much of an ad-
venturer or risk-taker—at least not physically. But I do love to
have fun, to play, to do new things. I love playing tennis, I'm
learning to play golf, and I want to do more and more of that
in my life, so I hang out with Richard every chance I get. My
family spends at least a week or ten days each year up on the
lake where he and his wife, Rishon, live in Idaho. A big part
of the 'why' of that, for me, is that Richard *makes* me have fun.
It's a value he's mastered, and one I want to cultivate.

"We share a number of values, as well," he told me.
"Richard is a leader. He's the owner and CEO of a Network
Marketing company. He's an author with the best book
about vision and self-motivation I've ever read, *Mach II with
Your Hair on Fire*. He has phenomenal integrity and a deep
and abiding love *for* and commitment *to* his people. In any
endeavor, he's a partner you can absolutely count on, and
there's not a smarter, sharper Network Marketing heart and
mind on the planet.

"All those *values*," he said, emphasizing the word, "are both
the current and currency of our relationship. I consider

Richard a best friend and I love him. Our relationship and friendship are based on our values. Do you see that?"

"Absolutely," I said, wishing more than anything for a number of *Richards* in my life.

"With Richard and me," The Greatest Networker continued, "our values fit together—those of his I admire and share, as well as the values he has that I don't but want more of in my life. Our values fit together to form the foundation of our relationship—do you see?"

"Yes, I do."

"Good. Now, the fit I just described is what I say you're looking for when you're prospecting for your Networking business. You're shopping for a business partner, someone you can trust, someone you'd really enjoy working with, playing with, teaching and learning from—yes?"

"That would be ideal."

"Why settle for less?"

"Why indeed?" I thought and said.

"*Alas and alack,*" he said with a faux melodramatic flair. "Sadly, most people in our business do not do that. They're focused on the money. It's a numbers game. Throw them up against the wall and see who sticks. Just get the application signed. Get them in and let's get on with it. Those and a dozen other false motivators have many to most Network Marketers failing to build successful businesses.

"Look," and he turned to look at me as he said it, "answer me as honestly as you can: Why in God's or anyone else's name would you want to bring somebody into your business who you were not *in love with?*"

* * *

SPONSOR ONLY PEOPLE you love—and who love you. It's
not practical, I thought to myself.

Nah, that's not true. Or I certainly want it not to be true.

Is it just too hard?

No, not really. It's not too hard. How could I say loving
people would be too hard?

Clearly I couldn't think of a good reason at that moment,
except . . . except what?

I had a sinking feeling.

Am I the kind of person people will love?

Before being asked to tell him what I was thinking—as I
was sure he was just about to do—I told him what I'd just
thought.

"Ah, *that* one," he said with a serious tone. "Very good.
Very good!"

What one? I thought, but didn't ask.

"You *are* a piece of work, my friend. That's great!" he exclaimed. "Well, you just tapped into the main vein of the
mother lode of what has kept humanity spinning its wheels
since the Garden of Eden. My guess is, *that's* the original
sin—at least it's one of the prime contenders.

"Am I the kind of person people can love? The essence of
that thought for you is the notion 'I'm not good enough' or
'I'm not enough'—yes?"

I nodded that it was.

"Imagine how many 'slings and arrows of outrageous
fortune' that one charming thought—in its two primary

35

incarnations—has unleashed on us poor mortals through the ages?" he said.

* * *

WE DROVE ALONG in silence for some time. I looked out the window directly to my right and watched the trees flying past in a gray blur. *I'm not good enough . . . not good enough . . . not good enough . . .* I repeated over and over in my mind.

I had the distinct sensation he was being silent on purpose, so I asked him if that was so.

"Yes. Seemed like a fine time to shut up," he smiled.

"I have some good news for you. Want it?" he asked, turning to see my face.

"You bet!" I said.

"You *made that up*."

"What do you mean? Made what up?"

"That bit about not being good enough—you made it up."

"I made it up," I repeated, not knowing if it was true or not, just playing around with saying it.

"Remember last night, that 'most uncomfortable' exercise I had you do?"

"Yes, I certainly do," I told him with conviction.

"So," he asked, "how do you *know* you're not good enough?" Pause.

"Got it!" I said. "I *did* make it up. I must have. Far out!" I was beginning to sense that *everything* I thought was simply made up.

"There is, however," he continued, interrupting my thoughts, "some bad news, as well."

"Wonderful," I said, "and what's *that?*"

"If you're anything like me—and I'm guessing you are—you will probably need to remind yourself that you made that all up a couple of hundred, perhaps thousands of times before it becomes a consistent habit of thought."

I groaned, sensing how right he was. "Well, that's certainly better than suffering the thought that I'm not good enough for the rest of my life."

"True," he replied. "Very true. And there's a way—actually a number of ways—to shift those balance scales. Remember them?"

I recalled the scales in my subconscious mind he'd described to me the past weekend I'd spent with him, like the ones blind justice holds, where all the positive and negative thoughts we've ever had are weighed out—and mostly the weight is negative.

He continued. "There are ways to shift those scales in your mind in favor of knowing that you are indeed far more than good enough."

"I am all ears," I told him.

"I noticed," he laughed, and I joined him. "What do you know about affirmations?"

"I know I think they're silly," I told him.

"That's a nice opinion," he said. "Want to change your mind about that?"

"Okay," I said with a smile. "I'll do that."

"An affirmation is a positive declaration—and incidentally," he interrupted himself, "I used to think they were silly, too. And since I know I made *that* up, I decided to make up something that made affirmations useful for me, rather than simply reject them. After changing my mind, I discovered that researchers in cognitive science were busy proving affirmations actually work and revealing the brain chemistry that explains how and why.

"Remember the bit I told you Thursday night about your smile? Same thing with affirmations; similar brain chemicals and electromagnetic impulses involved," he told me.

"Anyway, affirmations are positive phrases you can use to train your mind—mostly through the subconscious—away from negative thinking to something that will empower you. If you'll grant me there's research to back this up, as well as my own personal experience, would the idea that you can train your mind to empower rather than disempower you make sense?"

I told him it did.

"Good. Look over here," and he pointed to the lower left corner of the windshield in front of him. "Can you see that from where you're sitting?"

I leaned over a bit and saw what struck me first as some kind of magic trick. There, reflected in the car window, were white letters about an inch or so high, coming out of the dark background of the road in front of us forming the words:

I Experience

a Continuous

Flow of Prosperity

"Yes. I see it," I said excitedly. "That's really cool. What a great idea. Every time you drive your car you can read that message."

"Not exactly. It's even better than that. I assume you'd agree that driving down the road reading a sign in your windshield that took your eyes off the road could be a little dangerous—yes?"

"Hadn't thought of that," I admitted.

"More good news. You don't have to *read it,* not in the conventional sense. Fact is, 99.9989 percent of the time, you're focused on the road ahead—or looking in your mirrors—and while the sign is always there in your field of vision, your conscious mind isn't paying direct attention to the message.

"Of course, you'll notice it and read it to yourself frequently, but most of the time it just sits there beaming itself directly into your subconscious mind. That's the part of your mind that has been recording all of those 'not good enough' thoughts over and over again since you were a child. It's also the part of your mind where those positive/negative balance scales reside.

"I'll tell you," he confided, "I haven't always liked to drive all that much, but ever since I got that—oh, it's called an Auto Affirmation, by the way—ever since I got that sign, I've found I actually enjoy driving places. It's got to be either this message or this Mercedes—and that little sign is a lot less expensive."

"That's really neat," I told him.

"You know what's also fun—every time I go to a car wash or have someone valet park the car, I watch people notice the sign. They always look at me with this quizzical expression, and I get the sense they're thinking: 'What's that doing in an expensive car like this?' I know I'm assuming this, but it's happened so often I'm pretty sure that's what they're thinking. Anyway, when they say something to me about it, I say to them, 'How do you think I got this car?' I love it," he laughed.

"You can accomplish the same thing by writing down your own affirmations on three-by-five cards and placing them on your desk or wall where you work. You get that peripheral vision thing going on so the message is constantly sent to your subconscious mind.

"I'll tell you something else—and this is just my opinion *but* it's my experience, too—these affirmations work really quickly," he told me. "In fact, I think they can and do truly take hold in your mind in only 28 days. That's one complete cycle of the moon, and I've read the research that says that's the precise time it takes to change a habit. Make sense to you?"

"It does. You have any other tricks like Auto Affirmation you'd care to share?" I asked playfully, knowing full well he did. I had the thought that I'd never known anyone who knew as much as this man.

Once again, as if he could read my mind, he replied, "Sure. You know, people tell me I have a tremendous amount of knowledge, but I really don't think I know all that much. I recall a lot, that's true. Here's the secret: Everything I know, I learned from somebody else. That's true in every single part of my life, and it's especially true for all I know about Network Marketing."

"And I quote you to yourself," I said to him. "'If you knew what I know about Network Marketing, nothing in the world would prevent you from being successful.'"

"Did I say that?"

"You did."

"Well I got *that* from somebody else," he said. "As I re-member, it was originally said a little differently, and I've changed it to suit my own purpose. I think the exact remark was, 'If you knew what I know about Network Marketing, nothing would stop you from getting involved today!' Great line for prospecting, don't you think?"

"Couldn't have said it better myself," I told him, "In fact, I wish I *had* said it myself."

"You *can* say it yourself. I've forgotten who said it to me first, but it's a great line. Feel free to use it. We must be the only industry in the world that encourages plagiarism and *stealing* each other's material," he laughed. "That's part of having a duplicatable system.

"Oh my," he said with surprise and a laugh, "have we finally gotten back around on the guitar to *systems?*"

"I guess we have," I told him, "but you were about to share some other—what did I call them, *tricks?*—to help me change my mind. Can you talk about both?"

"Sure. What would you like first?"

The conversation continued. He talked about systems; about making money and trusting the process; about express-ing gratitude and appreciation; about bringing the industry together; and more. He talked until we arrived at the hotel—at 9:00 on the dot. He parked the car, and we walked through the door of the room where the training would take place.

CHAPTER THREE

Applause Training

THE LARGE HOTEL BALLROOM was set classroom style—long tables running parallel to the stage covered with white tablecloths, speckled with what I realized after taking a closer look were tiny gold foil hearts mixed together with little green dollar signs. What fun! Love and money. I'd never seen that before.

There was seating for perhaps 250 people, maybe more. Green and gold balloons rose up along the sides of the room and next to the stage. Even though it was a full hour before the training was to begin, there was some great uplifting music playing. Lots of drums and odd instruments. Great to dance to, I thought, with a feeling of anticipation. The festive room immediately brought a smile to my face.

All the tables and chairs faced the raised podium. A large company banner hung on the wall behind the stage. There was no lectern. No screen or overhead projector. No white or black board. In the center of the stage was only a high-backed director's chair next to a tall round table on which were a couple of bottles of water and a tall glass vase filled with a kaleidoscope of freshly-cut flowers.

Although I hadn't been in the business all that long, I realized this was not the usual setup for a Saturday training.

We were among the first to arrive, and the room started to fill up quickly. The Greatest Networker introduced me to our host, a smiling, ultra-bubbly redhead named Ruby, who—he explained to me in his introduction—had been involved in Network Marketing for 47 years!

"*Amazing!*" I thought out loud. "I didn't even know it was possible to have been in the business that long!" Just knowing Ruby, a very successful leader, had been around all that time deepened my regard for the industry.

Ruby gave me a hug, complete with a kiss on the cheek, and welcomed me so warmly I felt as if I'd known her forever. She introduced me to her husband, Ted, a tall distinguished man with silvery hair, and a number of the other people she was standing with. Then she excused herself from the group and went off towards the stage arm in arm with The Greatest Networker.

* * *

AT 10:00, THE room lights flashed on and off, the music stopped, and a young man bounded up on stage with a microphone in his hand and shouted a welcome "Good morning!" and "How are y'all today?" in a strong Southern accent.

He was greeted with applause and the group response, "Great!"

He introduced himself and told us about the agenda, when and where lunch was going to be served, how the day would go and by when we would be finished. Then he introduced Ruby and gave her his hand as she stepped up on to the stage. She gave him a big hug and a kiss on the cheek, like she'd given me, and took the microphone as he left the stage.

What a ball of fire she was—and she was clearly *having a ball*, as well.

She immediately started talking excitedly about what a wonderful business Network Marketing was that it could bring so many "lovely people" together who cared so much about each other, who loved what they were doing together and who were making such a contribution to the health and wealth of so many people.

I recalled while I was listening to her how, in the beginning, I heard people say such things in meetings and thought it sounded a little false or hollow. You know, put on—more hype than real. But boy, there wasn't a hint of that from Ruby. She was so sincere I could literally feel her conviction. It was clear she believed with every fiber of her being how wonderful Network Marketing, her company, her people, even this event here today really were.

I immediately remembered the new definition of belief The Greatest Networker had shared with me that night in the restaurant. It was clear to me that Ruby was being love with all she was doing and saying.

Is that why she seemed so *believable*, I asked myself?
And I answered, as well—yes, of course it was.

* * *

I BROUGHT MYSELF back to listening to Ruby.

"Today, you have a very special treat in store. You're going to be with a man whose vision has truly taken this industry a giant step forward. What he will share with you today are ideas and insights that will actually change the way you approach your business—and with that, your happiness and success throughout your life.

"He is a leader in his company—the top producer. He's an author, editor, million-dollar income earner and a mentor to so many leaders in our business. He is a global champion of Network Marketing, a true industry expert who has spoken throughout the United States and Canada, as well as in Australia, Malaysia, China, England, even Russia.

"And with all he has accomplished and all he has taught so many people, there's one primary thing I've learned from him that I will treasure forever: This business is about *love*—loving and being loved.

"Love is what we all want most, and love is what we can all give best. According to him, no matter what company we're with or what items we market and sell, our real product is love. And," Ruby said with a long yet smiling sigh that revealed her deep emotion, "I *love him* for that.

"If you get the chance," she continued, "ask him to talk about that. That's what we'll be doing today. He says he doesn't like to talk at people like other speakers—although he knows so much he can spend an hour answering one question. He prefers to talk *with* us. He insists that the best way to train is simply having a conversation with people. This is a man who knows—and speaks—the truth.

"My dear friends," Ruby said warmly, "it's an honor to introduce you to *my dear friend,* The Greatest Networker in the World."

The Greatest Networker jogged up the center aisle and jumped up on stage.

* * *

HE GOT HIS HUG and kiss from Ruby and stood taking in the applause, all the while holding her hand. He smiled, told the group "thank you" a couple of times, and seemed slightly, though genuinely, embarrassed by the attention. When the applause subsided, he began.

"Thank you," he said. "Thanks for having me here with you today. I appreciate that very much, and I appreciate each of you for being here.

"I'm intent on having today be valuable for you. I'm committed to your leaving here with at least one new $100,000 *a month* idea. Is that something that would interest you?" he asked the group.

"Sure. You bet. Yes!" came the responses.

"Great, let's start right away. How many of you would be interested in a simple, yet powerful, technique you can incorporate into all of your meetings and trainings that will instantly transform the excitement and energy level in the room, give monster recognition to your people, and make each and every one of you *feel fantastic*—how many of you would be interested in learning that, especially if it was easy to do?" he asked. "Raise your hands."

And the group—almost as one—did.

"Great!" he said again. "Let me ask you a question first. Think back to the applause you greeted Ruby with this morning: On a scale of one to ten—with ten being masterful, high energy, empowering, rock concert, *wow!*—how would you rate this morning's applause?" He asked and looked around the room.

"Five," one woman said.

"Seven," said another.

There were a number of threes and sixes, some fours and some twos.

"Okay," he said. "So it seems you all agree that there's room for improvement—yes?"

The audience agreed.

"Great," he told them. "Now, I want to show you an absolutely fail-safe way to generate masterful applause that will always rate a perfect ten. And, as I promised, the good news is, it's easy! First, let me ask another question. Who is applause for—the person or people on stage, or you, the audience?"

Most of the people seemed to agree it was for those on stage.

"Ah, good. Well, of course the people on stage get a great benefit from your applause. They feel appreciated and acknowledged, and that's really valuable in trainings and when people are brought up on stage to be recognized at your company conventions.

"But the fact is," he continued, "applause has a tremendous impact on all of you sitting out there. So, I want you to take your pulse right now. Just check out how you feel—*right now.* And when we've finished this exercise, I'm going to check in with you to see if you feel any difference. Okay?"

We agreed.

"I learned this technique from Russ DeVan when I saw him speak at Sandy Elsberg's *Bread Winner Bread Baker* seminar in Los Angeles," he told us. "Russ is a master Networker, a leader who's a million-dollar income earner—been in the business 20 years.

"When you master this technique—and you'll be able to do that today, guaranteed—I promise you that all your meetings and trainings will take on a whole new level of excitement and success.

"Now," he asked, "you agree that one of the important things for people in our business is recognition?"

The group agreed.

"And would you agree that when someone's up on stage, you, the audience, can positively impact their presentation by having them feel instantly wanted, important, and appreciated?"

The group agreed.

"Would you also agree with me that if each of you felt really excited to be here . . . if you were anticipating having just the *very best time ever* . . . if you were awake, alert, and having fun . . . would you agree that you'd feel happy, enthusiastic, and better than merely alive and well?" he asked.

Again, the group agreed.

"Great!" he exclaimed. "Here's how you can have all of that and more. All you have to do is clap you hands together *faster or harder* than the person sitting next to you. Can you do that?"

The audience laughed and agreed they could.

"Okay, I knew this was a *very* bright group, but that's pretty basic—just put your two hands together harder or faster than your neighbor. Would you be willing to try some advanced work with me this morning?"

And again the audience laughed and agreed.

"Cool," he said playfully.

"Okay, what you do is this: While you're clapping harder or faster than the people sitting next to you, turn to the one on the left and say something—anything. Then turn to the person on the right and say something. Nod your head up and down while you do this.

"By the way," he told the smiling audience, "it doesn't matter what you say. You could say something about your favorite sports team, the weather, tell a short joke—anything is fine. It really doesn't matter. See, all you want to do here is comment back and forth, smiling and nodding your head, while you clap harder or faster than the person sitting next to you. Have you got all of this? Are you ready to try it out?"

By this time, the entire audience was buzzing, smiling and laughing—and definitely *ready*.

"All right," he told them, still holding Ruby's hand. "In just a moment I'm going to introduce Ruby, and when I do I want you to give this applause business your very best effort. It's kind of a quiz, and I want you all to get A-pluses. Ready?" he asked.

We were.

"Ladies and gentlemen," he began with a ringmaster's voice, "I want you to meet and show your genuine love and enthusiasm for an *extraordinary woman* . . . a woman who's been in this business *for 47 years!* A top leader and a person I consider to be *The Greatest Networker in the World.* Ladies and gentlemen, your very own *Ru-uby.* . . ."

He took a quick step backwards, which had the effect of moving Ruby to the very front of the stage, and as he did this, the room literally exploded with applause. It was thunderous, like a huge wave crashing on the beach. People were clapping and turning to the left and right, talking and laughing and nodding their heads. Several people in the first couple of rows stood up and suddenly it seemed as if the entire room jumped to its feet as one.

It was *amazing!*

Ruby was beaming. The people were applauding, laughing, and talking back and forth together. Indeed, you could actually feel the increased energy and excitement in the room.

"*That was great!*" The Greatest Networker exclaimed as the noise of the crowd subsided and people started to sit down again. "Twelve on a scale of one to ten! *Fantastic!*

"Now," he said, "look at Ruby's face. How do you think she feels right now? Do you think she's juiced and jazzed by your acknowledgment? Do you think she's going to give you her best better-than-ever today?

"*You bet!*" he answered his own question as the audience agreed.

"And how do you all feel?" he asked us. "Are you more alive than when we started? Do you feel pumped up—even just a little? Was that fun for you? Doesn't that make you feel great?"

Again, the group agreed as one.

"You people are amazing. Where did that standing thing come from? I was saving that for some really advanced work—if I was ever invited back," he told us with a laugh. "A standing ovation! That's Ph.D.-level stuff. You guys are incredible!"

Have you ever heard the expression "Had them right in the palm of his hand"? Well, he did. This audience—me included—was his.

* * *

HE LEANED OVER to give Ruby a kiss on the cheek, then walked with her to the edge of the platform, leaning over and guiding her down the steps. Then, he walked back across the stage and lifted himself up into the director's chair. He opened one of the bottles of water, took a drink, set the bottle on the table and let out a deep breath as he settled into the chair crossing his legs and folding his hands around one raised knee.

I don't know how long he sat like that in silence, looking at the faces in the audience before he spoke. It was probably only 15 or 20 seconds, but it seemed a long time.

"You know," he began, "I think Network Marketers are just the best looking people in the world," he said and laughed a small version of his booming laugh. "So how can I help you?"

The audience was silent. Some people looked at each other. Others seemed to feel restless. Clearly nobody was going to be the first one to speak first.

"Ah," he said, "I've been in a predicament like this before. Nobody needs help. Your businesses are all going perfectly. Is that true for you?" he asked with another deep and lasting laugh.

He climbed out of his chair, walked to the front of the platform and promptly sat himself down on the front of the stage, dangling his feet over the edge.

"Look," he said, directly searching the faces of a number of people in the first couple of rows. "I can sit up here and talk at you all morning. I don't know about you, but I don't care for that. Fact is, after the years I've spent in this business, I'm kind of speakered out," he laughed.

"There are a couple of things going on here," he told us. "First, I don't presume to know what you want to know from me. So I'm asking you. That way, I'm certain I'm speaking to you and what's on your agenda.

"The other way, I'm only speaking about what I want— and I do *that* all the time. Speaking about what you want, how I can help you, is much more interesting. I've been with me so long and talked about my favorite topics so many times, they're getting a little boring," he laughed.

"The other thing is," he continued, his eyes traveling the audience, focusing on as many people as possible, "I believe that life is a conversation. Literally, that we create our lives—and our work—in conversation. Please, think about that for a moment. Life is a *conversation*." He sat quietly as we considered the thought.

"Tell me," he asked, breaking the silence of thought, "How many of you believe in the old Network Marketing adage 'Keep it simple and duplicatable'?"

Many people nodded, said aloud that they agreed or raised their hands.

"Good," he said. "Me, too.

"So, let me make a statement and see if you agree. A brilliant trainer and friend of mine, Chris Majer, turned me on to this. He's taught leadership and teamwork to Fortune 500 executives, Green Berets, Army Rangers, and Olympic athletes. Here's what Chris taught me: There are only three things you do in Network Marketing. *Only* three," he said.

"First, you use your body. True?" he asked, looking around the group.

I could see that people were with him, yet they didn't know exactly where he was going. I certainly didn't, so I listened even more closely.

"Since you use your body and depend on it working properly, you've got to take care of it," he said. "In all my years in this business, I haven't seen one dead person become successful," he smiled and the audience chuckled.

"In fact," he continued, "although there are many heartwarming stories of people who've become quite ill and whose upline and downline helped them build a successful business even while they were bedridden, that's pretty rare—don't you think?" he asked, and we all got the point.

"Your health is crucial to being successful in this business," he said with real passion in his voice. "You can't grow a big organization if your body is too tired to go to meetings and trainings, or if your body cannot pick up the phone at three in the afternoon because it lacks vitality and energy. You won't succeed in this or any business if your body is sick all the time, suffering from colds that prevent you from prospecting, headaches that stop you from making follow-up phone calls, or a bad back so much in pain that it keeps you from going to events.

"I'm speaking about your total body. If you're not mentally and emotionally healthy, if your body is angry and can't get along with people, or your body is so worried and afraid that you won't take a risk or be willing to adventure into something unknown, you'll never succeed in Network Marketing," he said.

"And if your body is greedy—you know what that means: You want more than you think you deserve—or selfish, if your body's ego is out of control, if your behavior is out of integrity, you will not become a leader in this business. You may succeed for a short time, but that success won't last." Now everybody was hanging on his words.

"This industry has a natural structure of integrity that honors people and their values, and if you are crazy, manipulative, or self-obsessed, it will *spit you out!*" he said forcefully. "People like that are not healthy, and they do not succeed in Network Marketing.

"You see," he said, slipping off the front of the stage and pacing up the aisles, looking from face to face to face, "you absolutely must have a healthy body to succeed in this business. If you don't, you can't. You've got to take care of your entire body—your physical body, mental body, emotional body, and spiritual body. Is there anyone here who doesn't think that's true?" he asked.

No one raised a hand.

"You are all fortunate because your company offers some of the finest health products in the entire world. But even with your superb products, you've got to take great care of your diet," he told us. "You can't exist on meat and sugar and highly-refined junk food, then grab some herbs and nutritional supplements—*no matter how great they are*—and make a lifetime of carelessness all better.

"Forget the burger. Grab a salad. Pick potato chips cooked in good, clean oil. Spend the extra money and shop at a natural food store. Avoid the pesticides and the artificial ingredients. You just know something that kills all those bugs doesn't belong in your system. Buy organic. It costs more, and that's fine because *you're worth it*.

"And *exercise!*" he added passionately. "Every day. Something. *Anything!* How many of you honestly live *active* lifestyles?" A few hands were raised, but not many.

"I know. Me, too," he admitted, shaking his head. "So, I make myself active. I make the time to play tennis and golf. I'm fortunate enough to have a gym in my home, so I work out two or three times a week.

"If you and I lived on a farm or worked hard like our grandparents did," he continued, "there'd be no need for us to exercise. That demanding physical lifestyle would be enough. But life on the phone isn't life on the farm. Driving from one place to another in our car-qualified rides sitting on our butts won't cut it.

"Exercise is just a fun and interesting way to give your body the work it needs to stay healthy, vital, and strong.

"I highly recommend lifting weights," he said, putting up his hand to quell resistance. "I know, I know. The first thought you have is some bulging Saturday morning no-neck wrestlemaniac—right?

"I promise you, lifting light weights for 30 minutes—twice or thrice a week—will do more for your health than you can imagine. You don't have to be *A-a-arnold*," he laughed, "but your muscles need to be lean and strong and flexible. If you play with light weights and do the movements a number of times until you say to yourself, 'That's it, that's enough,' you'll do just fine. You'll see improvement quickly. Your body will love you for it. You'll look great! Feel even better!

"Please, my friends," he said, "whether you consider your body a temple or a tool, diet and exercise are really, really important. So, 'just do it'—okay?

"Great, so you use your body. The other two things you do, the *only* other two things you do in this business are: You *speak* and you *listen*."

After a moment, he asked us, "Please, turn to the person sitting next to you—to the right, left, or someone sitting behind or in front of you—and talk about this for a moment. Besides using your body, you only do two things in Network Marketing. You *speak*, and you *listen*. Please, discuss this for a couple of minutes with your partner. Start now."

And with that, he jumped back up on the stage, climbed into his chair, took a sip of his water, and watched the people in the room intently.

CHAPTER FOUR

Stop, Look, and Listen

THE ROOM HAD been buzzing with people speaking back and forth for perhaps three or five minutes when The Greatest Networker clapped his hands together twice and spoke in a voice, that boomed out over all our talking, "Stop. Now. Please."

The talking started to fall off, but many people were still at it.

"*Stop. Now!*" He said clapping his hands again.

"Can you imagine how difficult it is to get a room full of Network Marketers to *stop* talking?" he asked those of us in the front row close to him with a laugh. "Stop! Stop! *Stop!*" he implored, and the group settled down to silence.

"Thank you," he said. "So, what do you know about this speaking and listening business? Is it true for you—is that all you do? Did you discover anything interesting from your conversations just now?"

He looked around the room for a response. There was none.

"Okay, my friends," he said, now standing at the front edge of the stage, "Let me share something with you—and I'm saying this because I have the sense that some of you might disagree with me, but you're not willing to speak about it.

"Let me ask you this—a show of hands, please—from which do you learn the most: That which you *agree* with? Or that which you *disagree* with?

"Who among you learns most from agreement? Raise your hands," he said, raising his hand high above his head.

A few people did. Not many.

"Who learns most from disagreement?"

More people raised their hands this time.

"Now, a whole bunch of you didn't raise your hands at all," he said to the group. "You must be the shy ones. Tell me, how many of you are really shy people—raise your hands."

Nearly a third of the audience had their hands raised when he laughed and said, "As Tom 'Big Al' Schreiter says, 'Shy people would *never* raise their hands.' What *are* you guys *doing*? Did you all just have a comfort zone breakthrough?"

We all smiled and some people laughed. He had the same great way of making an entire room feel at ease as he did when it was just the two of us together. I immediately had the thought that he could probably have the whole group feel pretty uncomfortable, too—and just as easily.

"When you agree with what I'm saying, that's nice," he told us, "and I'm using 'nice' here as in 'Have a *nice day*' nice. Really—*who cares?* 'Have a *nice* day.' No thanks, I have more ambitious plans!"

The group laughed with him.

"When you agree with me," he continued, "that might make *you* feel good. You might even think it makes *me* feel good. And by the way," he added, "feeling *good* isn't *feeling* anything. It's just a thought you have and *call* a feeling. It would really be more accurate to say, 'Oh, I *think* good.'

"So apart from a fleeting thought of *feeling nice* for the moment, there's not all that much real value in agreement. I certainly haven't made a difference for you. I haven't contributed anything new to what you know, or even what you don't know—have I?" he asked, and looked around for the clearly obvious answer.

"It's the stuff you disagree with that has real, even lasting and perhaps life-changing, value. Yet what do we do with disagreement? We throw the object/subject we don't agree with away. We reject it. 'I disagree with that, so I don't have to look any deeper.' I'm asking you to use a different approach."

He stood silently for a moment, then said, "Let me read you something about doing things differently."

He reached for his notebook, and put his glasses on as he turned the pages. When he reached what he wanted, he looked up at us, then back down at the page and began to read.

"This is from a wonderful little book *you²*," he told us, "by Dr. Price Pritchett. It goes like this. . . .

I'm sitting in a quiet room at the Millcroft Inn.
A peaceful little place hidden back among the pine
trees about an hour out of Toronto. It's just past

noon, late July, and I'm listening to the desperate
sounds of a life-or-death struggle going on just a few
feet away.

There's a small fly burning out the last of its short
life's energies in a futile attempt to fly through the
glass of the windowpane. The whining wings tell the
poignant story of the fly's strategy—try harder.

But it's not working.

The frenzied effort offers no hope for survival.
Ironically, the struggle is part of the trap. It is impossible for the fly to try hard enough to succeed at breaking through the glass. Nevertheless, this little insect
has staked its life on reaching its goal through raw effort and determination.

This fly is doomed. It will die there on the win-
dowsill.

Across the room, ten steps away, the door is open.
Ten seconds of flying time and this small creature
could reach the outside world it seeks. With only a
fraction of the effort now being wasted, it could be
free of this self-imposed trap. The breakthrough possibility is there. It would be so easy.

Why doesn't the fly try another approach, something dramatically different? How did it get so locked
in on the idea that this particular route, and deter-
mined effort, offer the most promise for success?
What logic is there in continuing until death, to seek
a breakthrough with 'more of the same'?

No doubt this approach makes sense to the fly. Re-
grettably, it's an idea that will kill it.

'Trying harder' isn't necessarily the solution to achieving more. It may not offer any real promise for getting what you want out of life. Sometimes, in fact, it's a big part of the problem.

If you stake your hopes for a breakthrough on trying harder than ever, you may kill your chances for success.

"Here's my request for you today," he said to the group, sitting back up in his chair and regarding us earnestly. "Do something different. Look for those things you disagree with. Those are the ideas which are really the most important for you. That's the place where a breakthrough will come from.

"And please," he implored, holding up his hand, "I am not asking you to know that what I say is true. Please don't do that. Just listen. Let the words and ideas in. Put it on like you're trying on a suit or a new pair of shoes."

He climbed off his chair and stood sideways to the audience pretending we were one of those three-sided, full-length mirrors as he cocked his head to the left and right and then turned as if looking at himself and the clothes he was trying on. "Hmmm, this is not a bad idea. Looks pretty good if I do say so myself," he said with a laugh, unbuttoning his jacket and adjusting his sleeve admiringly in the imaginary reflection of the audience.

"Yes, I think I'll take it. No, no, I don't care how much it costs. I'm a successful Network Marketer," he said with a wave of his hand. "I'm mastering my possibilities. Here's my credit card." And the group laughed.

"What I'm asking you to do," he told us, "is what a mentor of mine, Mike Smith of the Center For Leadership Design, who teaches *The Power 2 Create* course, once asked me to do when he was coaching us. For the moment, set aside your opinions about what I'm saying. Just suspend your evaluations, assessments, judgments, comparisons, what your experience has taught you is true, all your likes and dislikes . . . put all of that and those away—just for today—and let that new thought or idea you hear into your heart and mind. Try it on. Wear it for a bit. See if it fits. You don't *have* to *buy* it.

"Hey!" he exclaimed. "This is Network Marketing. I'm not trying to *convince* you of anything. I'm in the *sorting* business," he said smiling and getting smiles in return.

"So, do you accept my request?" he asked, sitting down again in his tall chair. "I'm asking you to try these ideas on—especially the ones you disagree with at first—again, just for today. See if they fit. If they do—great! Please use them. And if not, *please*, before you leave; take back the opinion you came in with—okay?

"Is there anyone who does not accept my request?" He scanned the group. No hands were raised.

"Great. What do you think about this speaking and listening business? Is there anything else—besides, of course, using and taking care of your body—is there anything else you do in Network Marketing?"

A number of people spoke up from their seats. When they did, he requested they stand and asked them their names. I noticed—and filed away for future reference—that he used their first names frequently in the interactions he had with each of them.

Mostly, people gave examples of instances they thought were not speaking or listening, like thinking or handing out a video like *Brilliant Compensation*. He listened carefully to each one, then asked the whole group what we thought. Was this or that speaking or listening—or was it both? In the end, nobody had come up with anything that wasn't either speaking or listening.

"Ladies and gentlemen of the jury," he said, with his hands spread apart and a deep bow, "my case is taking a rest." He smiled, then continued.

"So, let's say—and please remember, this isn't *the truth. . . .*" He reminded us this was simply something we were *trying on* for the moment, just to see if it fit. "Let's say that after the use of your body, all you do is speak and listen. That's in keeping with 'keep it simple and duplicatable'— yes?"

We agreed.

"So, when you're training your people, and when you're learning the business yourself, those are *the* two fundamental areas for you to focus on," he said.

"Now, of the two, which one—speaking or listening—is the skill that's missing for you?"

A man in front raised his hand. He stood, introduced himself as George, and said, "Well, it's not really *missing*, but I find I have trouble talking to people. I'm not comfortable doing that. I'd say speaking is the skill I need to develop most." He sat down.

"George," The Greatest Networker said, "would you stand again, please, so we can talk?" George stood up and The Greatest Networker continued. "George, here's what I mean when I ask 'What's missing?' What I'm asking by using that question is: What's missing that, if it was put into the mix of actions you're taking, would produce the result you're after? Is that more clear, George?"

"Yes," George said. "I understand."

"So," The Greatest Networker went on, "is what you're telling me, George, that if you had a better handle on speaking, you'd be a more successful Network Marketer?" As he asked the question, he moved from his chair to sit again on the front edge of the stage closer to the audience.

"Sure," George responded, adding, "I'm just not comfortable speaking with people, especially strangers."

"I understand, George," The Greatest Networker said. "That used to be so for me, too. I know that's hard for people to believe since here I am up on stage. I often speak in front of thousands of people. Yet it's really been only recently that I became comfortable talking with people. I'm naturally one of those shy people who wouldn't raise his hand," he said with a laugh. "You, too, George?"

George nodded with a knowing smile.

"The key for me," he continued, "and I tell you this because I've watched this very same approach work for literally hundreds and thousands of people, wasn't in my speaking. Not really—and of course, speaking was involved. But, George, the real breakthrough for me came in my *listening*.

"Let me tell you a great story. . . ." The Greatest Networker told George and the group the anecdote he'd shared with me over dinner at Hiroshi's two nights before about the psychiatrist on the airplane who only asked questions.

66

When he'd finished his story, The Greatest Networker asked, "So, George, imagine you're the psychiatrist and I'm your seatmate—okay?"

George agreed.

The Greatest Networker smiled. "Now, do you see how I might find you to be the most interesting person I'd ever met—even though all *you* did was ask *me* questions?"

"Yes, I do," George responded.

"Good. And why is that?"

"Why would I think you were so interesting?" George asked back.

"Yup," The Greatest Networker replied.

"Well," said George, "I guess . . . because you were so interested in me."

"You guess? Aren't you very sure that's *exactly* why you'd find me so darn interesting, George?" he asked.

"I guess . . . no, no," George said, stopping himself. "Yes. You were interested in me, so I thought you were an interesting person, too."

"We're all like that," said The Greatest Networker, speaking to the entire group. "As human beings we live in a relative world. That's the real theory of relativity. Everything's *relative* for us.

"Now, I'm not out to prove Einstein wrong here," he laughed. "Even after all these years, $E = mc^2$ is still solid science. My point is that people are reciprocal. I like people who like me. I *love* people who love me. And I usually don't care much for people who can't stand me," he said with a big smile.

"Is that true for any of you, as well?" he asked us, raising his hand. And, of course, we agreed.

"It's all *relative*," he repeated. "You and I relate best to people who are relating to us. And the best way of relating to another human being is to *listen* to them. *Really* listen. And you know what, my friends?" he asked, then answered in a loud and powerful voice which emphasized every word: "*Nobody is listening—nobody!*"

* * *

HE SAT ON the stage looking at us. Thirty seconds, maybe even a minute passed, and he didn't say a word. Then he repeated, softly, "Nobody's listening. . . ."

He jumped off the front of the stage and walked over to the right side of the room, speaking the entire time. "Has this ever happened to you? You're walking down the street and you see someone you've met before approaching you. You smile—you're happy to see her. As you come close to each other, she says with a smile, 'Hi, how are you?' And then . . ."—as he said this he turned around facing in the opposite direction, stretching out his hand and faltering forward as if he'd reached for something and missed—"she *walks right on past you!*

"There you are about to tell her how you are—how your boss is a pain in a number of your body parts, how you wish you'd been earning more money, how you're really skiing much better than you were last year (must be those new parabolic skis—Boy, aren't they something!), how your daughter got in a car accident and her '89 Volvo is probably totaled, and no, no, she's fine, thanks. No big deal. Just an expense you hadn't planned for and really can't afford . . . and *you're talking to the woman's back!* She's halfway down the block! She's not listening! *She didn't really want to know how you were at all!*

"Ever happened to you?" Before we could answer he held up his hand saying, "Wait. That was a bad example, I know. I should have used a man instead of a woman. A woman would always stop and talk. Women do that. Isn't that so, women?" The women all agreed (as I'm sure that he knew they would), and we all smiled.

"How many of you have ever finished someone else's sentence for them?" he asked, raising his hand and watching as hands were raised throughout the audience.

"*You're not listening,*" he said.

"How many of you cut people off, because you already *know* what they're going to say?"

And again hands shot up throughout the group.

"*You're not listening,*" he said, again. "That's mind reading. That's not listening. How many of you get into conversations with other people where you just can't wait for your turn? You're just waiting for them to stop talking so you can tell 'em what *you* think—just hanging on until they take a breath, 'cause *you can't wait* to share your better idea. Any of you ever do *that?*" he asked.

He didn't even wait for a show of hands this time.

"*You're not listening,*" he said immediately.

"Any of you married?" Three quarters of the room raised their hands.

"Your spouse knows *you're not listening,*" he laughed, and we joined him.

"Any of you have kids? *They* know you're not listening, and you know they haven't heard a word *you've* said in years! Why else do you have to tell them everything five times? Stop. Stop. Stop. Stop. *Stop!*" The entire audience was now laughing and agreeing, shaking and nodding their heads.

* * *

"MY FRIENDS," he said softly, taking his seat back on the front edge of the stage, "*you . . . do . . . not . . . listen*. Nobody does. Well, *almost* nobody—99.9989 percent of the people we talk to are not listening to us. The front porch light's on. Dog's barking. But *nobody's home*. . . . And it's not because we're bad people. It comes with being human beings—that's all. Were any of you taught to listen in school? How many college-credit hours did you get from taking Listening 101?" he asked.

Of course, none of us had or had any.

"I know some of you in management or sales positions have probably taken something like an 'Active Listening' course—those six-hour affairs where the company brings in a $5,000-a-day 'communications expert' to show you how to *look like* you're listening. That's not what I'm speaking about," he laughed.

"Listening, the kind of listening I'm talking about and call 'Creative Listening,' is very rare in our world today. Most of what passes for listening isn't," he told us. "It's Reactive Listening—not Creative Listening.

"There are two parts to Creative Listening: Open Listening and Listening By Design. The two parts of Reactive Listening are Closed Listening and Listening By Default.

"With Closed Listening, you're not open to what's being said—and listening, like a parachute, works only when it's open. . . . Listening By Default is listening that comes from your past. It is your programmed listening—it's you listening on automatic, computerized like a laptop by your past opinions of life and work and all your experiences of people and events. It's not listening by choice. It's listening that's not *responseable*. It doesn't empower you or others.

"Let me tell you a story," he said thoughtfully, "that illustrates this kind of Reactive Listening we have for others. In this example, which comes from Dr. Stephen Covey and his wonderful, all-time bestseller *The Seven Habits of Highly Effective People*, you'll see a powerful demonstration of the Closed Listening and Listening By Default that I've been speaking about.

"One Sunday morning," he began, "Dr. Covey was taking a ride on the subway in New York City. During the week, these subways are packed with people hurrying here and there, but on Sundays the folks are pretty laid-back and really quite peaceful—*New York Times*, cappuccino, bagel and lox.

"The train pulls into a station, the doors slide open, and into the car *explode* these two *wild* children," he said, jumping off the stage with his arms flying in the air and his voice rising. "These kids are *bouncing off the walls* of the subway car. Their father follows them in and sits himself down next to Covey, seemingly oblivious to anything else going on in the world.

"These kids are literally out of control—they're running back and forth, knocking people and their belongings around. They even grab one lady's newspaper right out of her hands!

71

"Now," he said to the audience, "what do you think is the Reactive Listening Covey has for these children's father?"

"He's not responsible," one man said.

"He doesn't know how to control his children," a woman suggested.

"A bad parent," said another.

"*Right,*" The Greatest Networker said. "This guy's a real loser. What an irresponsible father—right?"

And most of the audience agreed.

"Finally," The Greatest Networker said, spreading his hands and throwing them up and out in a gesture of exasperation, "Covey turns to the man and, clearly angry, says, '*Look!* Your kids are disturbing *everybody*. You've got to take responsibility for their actions and *get them under control now!*'"

"Well," The Greatest Networker said, his voice becoming hushed and soft, "the guy lifts his head up for the first time since he sat down, looks over at Covey, shuts his eyes, shakes his head slowly back and forth and says, 'I'm so sorry. I didn't realize what they were doing. We just came from the hospital where their mother died this morning. I guess they don't know how to handle it—I know I don't. . . .'"

The Greatest Networker sat down silently, letting the story sink in. And sink in—I could tell—it did for every one of us.

After a while, he continued. "The Reactive Listening Dr. Covey had—and I'm sure this was the same for everybody else in that subway car—was that this guy was an irresponsible jerk! That was the *way it was*. That was his *listening*.

"But Dr. Covey got some new information which changed his listening 180 degrees! He moved *immediately* from a listening of disgust to one of compassion, from a listening of anger to one of love, asking instead, 'My friend, *how can I help?*'

"Reactive Listening doesn't lead to anything but people talking to themselves inside their own heads—listening through their own opinions and interpretations, agreeing, disagreeing, mind reading, being right, making the other person wrong, judging, evaluating, comparing, arguing. . . . When Reactive listening, Listening By Default, is all there is, there can be no *real* conversation . . . no *real* learning . . . no *real* sharing . . . no communion . . . no intimacy . . . no partnership . . . no friendship. . . . There can be *no relationship at all.*"

He let that last part hang in the air while he got up on stage to take a drink of water.

"My friends," he interrupted the silence he'd created, "as Network Marketers, you're in the *relationship* business. That's what you do for a living—you create and maintain *relationships*. You grow that relationship into a *friendship*. When you take that friendship into a *partnership*, we call it sponsoring. Then you transform your partnerships through leverage into tens, hundreds, even thousands more partnerships to create an organization. You do *that* with *leadership*.

"And you do all of this through speaking and listening. I want to take on the listening side of the coin first, because it's the harder of the two to really understand. With speaking," he continued, "there is a shortcut I can show you which every one of you can learn and use immediately, as of today. With practice, you'll become a master of it in a month—perhaps less.

"We'll get to that in a bit. First, I brought along an article for you to read. Ruby, would you please have a couple of your people pass these to everyone?" he asked, holding out a stack of copies he brought with him for her to hand out.

"Thanks," he said. "What I'd like to do is take a 20-minute break—that should be enough time for you to refresh yourselves and give the article a quick read before we continue—yes?"

"Great," he said as we agreed. "I'll see you back here in 20 minutes. And thanks—in advance," he said, "for being on time. I appreciate you."

(Following is a copy of the article he gave us to read.)

STOP, LOOK & LISTEN

11 reasons why you can't hear
what other people are saying

Research has shown that people are listening only 25 percent of the time and they *make up* the rest of what they think or say they hear. This is a habit most people have in our world today, in and out of Network Marketing.

The cost is clear for the "non-listener." He doesn't learn what there is to know. Relationship becomes a no-possibility. Education fails. Success eludes.

And what do you suppose this phenomenon of *not* being heard creates for the speaker?

It's a game where both sides lose.

Not listening is the classic *Lose-Lose*.

So, why don't we listen?

Why don't we hear what other people are saying?

There are 11 reasons. (Perhaps you can come up with number 12 or even 13.) And each and every one of these explanations has to do with the person doing something other than hearing what's being said, or what's called "Reactive Listening"—a kind of non-listening where, for one or more of the reasons listed, the person does not hear what is being said.

If you can identify your "Reactive Listening," i.e., what you are doing instead of really listening to the other person, you can begin to change the outcome of any communication for the better—even for the very best—by "Creative Listening."

So, when you get the first sense that you are not hearing someone (or understanding what you've read, or . . .), **Stop.** Take a **Look,** and see what you're doing instead. Then, you can choose to change what you're doing . . . **& Listen** openly, creatively.

Here's the list of 11 reasons why we don't hear what other people are saying:

When you find you're not listening, it's because you're . . .

- **Comparing**—Here's the real "death of a salesman." Comparison is competition, and you never want to compete with your customers or prospects—or your friends and family. Is what's being said *better* or *not as good as* something else you've heard? To cash in

75

on the coin of a popular phrase: *Fogetaboutit*. What you're forgetting about is *being right*. Who cares? It's a conversation! Just listen. And of course, stay away from any assessments about the messenger, and focus simply and completely on hearing his or her message.

- **Derailing**—Speaking of messages, the easiest way to deliver a clear, "I don't care about what you're saying (and, therefore, you!)" message to someone is to change the subject, knocking the other person off-track before she's finished. If you're unsure if she's done speaking, a great question to ask is, "Are you complete?" Or, "Have you said all you want to about that?" Now, change to another topic if you want. Better yet, don't *you* change the subject, let the other person do it. If you just can't stand one more second of that particular conversation, simply ask the other person's permission. "Bob, I'd like to move to a new subject. Is that okay with you?"

- **Dreaming**—"Excuse me. What did you say?" Or, "Would you repeat that?" Or, "What? Oh, sorry, I wasn't listening." *Great!* What's the communication there? Clearly, the speaker feels she's not important—maybe she even feels dismissed by you. *Not good.* Sometimes, you'll want to think about something someone has just said. Fine. Stop the conversation right there and then and say, "Wait a minute, Mary, I want to think about what you just said." Saying *that* is a great acknowledgment. The other person will both *respect* you and *love* you for it!

76

- **Fighting**—What could be more disturbing, and off-putting, than to hear your conversation partner say, "My dog's better than your dog"—or any variation on that playground theme? If you want to make a sure and fast enemy, disagree, disapprove, challenge, belittle, begrudge, disbelieve, put-down, or power-over the person who's talking. If you have the thought that what they're saying is "wrong," fine. Tell them you heard them and express what your own thought is. Disagreeing is part of communication, and it's only okay when the other side's been heard *first*.

- **Filtering**—We are all a product of our own unique education. It's hard work not to force what we hear others say through the filter of personal experiences, attitudes, positions, points of view, and opinions. But when you do that, are you truly *hearing* them? Or is what the other person has just said being held up to the gold standard of your very special, one-of-a-kind judgment and evaluation? Set your editorial commentary aside when you're listening. If you don't, all you'll ever hear is yourself.

- **Identifying**—"I can identify with that. . . . You're just like me. . . . Great minds think alike. . . ." Well, actually great minds disagree more often than not. That's how great minds grow great: They explore different ideas, challenge their own perceptions, entertain new thoughts and directions. Of course, it's fun to discover a like-minded or similar-feeling/thinking friend. However, beware and be aware of how you listen from a place of *agree* or *disagree*. If you can only hear what you identify with, you may end up lonely and ignorant. Unless, of course, you can identify with everything and everyone. And when you truly listen, *you can!*

- **Interpreting**—Here's a profound, and for many, perplexing truth: We make it all up. When someone says, "Blue," what color comes to your mind? Do you suppose it's a different shade, tint, hue of blue from mine? *Everything* is an interpretation. Even two scientists observing the same precise experiment can reach differing conclusions. For example, take this question: "Is this like Amway?" And this answer: "Absolutely not!" And this response: "Gosh, that's too bad. I'd love to learn about Amway!" The 11th Commandment: Thou Shall Not Interpret. Instead, just listen and find out what the speaker really *means*.

- **Mind Reading**—Oscar-winning director and playwright Mike Nichols said, "You'll never really know what I mean and I'll never know exactly what you mean." So, why try? Clearly, knowing what someone else is thinking is, well, *crazy!* We cannot read each other's minds. We cannot know another's thoughts and feelings. Oh, at times we may be very empathetic and intuitive with one another, absolutely "on the same wave-length." And it's always best to *ask*. We all enjoy the mind-reading magician, but is he who you really want to be—or, for that matter, want as a business partner?

- **Placating**—When someone continuously nods her head, agreeing with everything you say, how does that make you feel: Secure and at ease? Usually, it makes people's skin crawl! It's the kind of thing that's given "nice" such a bad name. Avoiding disagreement or conflict by putting on a people-pleasing personality actually sends people in just the opposite direction—they lose trust in you and don't feel safe with you. If you're intent on being happy, smile and listen. (You'll find it's impossible to have a negative thought with that big smile on your face. Try it.)

- **Plotting**—If you already have a *plot* in mind for the conversation you're having—like the structure of a novel or a play—you're not listening. If this is the case, you can't truly hear the other person. You're too involved in directing the conversation to fit with and stick to your plot. From a slightly more "sinister" angle, *plotting* can also be used as a term describing those times when a person has a "hidden agenda"—a secret scheme for controlling the outcome of the conversation. In either instance, creating authentic conversation is an illusion. If you've already written the plot, it will be impossible for the other person to be genuinely heard.

- **Rehearsing**—You cannot hear someone, even just a little bit, when you're thinking about what you're going to say next. There's clearly some of the "Fighter" here. A listener who's more interested in themselves and what they have to say communicates powerfully and immediately to the other person, leaving him feeling not cared for and at times even violated. As Stewart Emery said beneath the title of his brilliant book, *Actualizations*, "You Don't Have to Rehearse to Be Yourself."

All you have to do is *Listen*.

CHAPTER FIVE

Where Do You Live?

W ELCOME BACK," The Greatest Networker called out loudly from the stage. "Take your seats, please.

"According to my watch," he said, holding his wrist out in front of him as the last group of people were sitting down, "we're starting about six minutes late. I acknowledge that we're not on time, and I apologize for that.

"I especially offer an apology to those of you who were here on time. Tom Schreiter, who wrote the 'Big Al' books, pointed out once when we were in Australia together how unfair it is to penalize people who show up on time by waiting for the latecomers. I always intend to start on time. Sometimes, I don't make it, and I apologize.

"So what was the most interesting thing about the *Stop, Look & Listen* article you read? Did any of you see yourself in some of the descriptions of the 11 ways people don't listen?"

A number of people in the audience shared with the group what they'd identified as their own Reactive Listening.

As he finished calling on the last person, The Greatest Networker said, "I think you're beginning to see just how important this business of listening can be. Please, under-stand—*Creative Listening*," and he strongly emphasized the words, "may be the most powerful, personal, and profes-sional skill of all. That's certainly true for me—in my ca-reer *and* in my life.

"And look," he added, "listening is a *skill*. Because it is a skill, you can develop your competence in that area. With training and practice, you can become a master listener. Get yourself a teacher and remember how you get to Carnegie Hall: *Practice, practice, practice*.

"There are a number of brilliant people and organizations I've learned about listening from," he told us. "My first expo-sure was *The Communication Course* offered by the people who created the Forum and worked with Werner Erhard. I also studied for a bit with an amazing man named Arnold Segal who offered an intensive course of study called *The Conversation*.

"I think a great deal of the material these people taught began with an extraordinary man named Fernando Flores. His organization is called Logonet. Flores was a political pris-oner in Chile where he had formerly been a cabinet minis-ter. He and his family were persecuted and brutally treated, and Amnesty International got him out of jail and brought him to America. The day after he arrived, he was teaching a seminar—an incredible, incredible man whose understanding of language brings a whole new dimension to speaking and listening.

"And in my opinion," he said, leaning back with his hands tucked in his jacket pockets, "*the* foremost authority, teacher, and coach on this planet in the area of listening is a lady named Carol McCall. I've studied with Carol, and she is both a mentor and dear friend. She offers a three-day course entitled *The Empowerment of Listening*. She also has a tape series by the same name, which I absolutely recommend to each and every one of you."

* * *

"GEORGE," HE SAID, calling on the man he'd spoken with earlier, "after what you've read and what's just been said, do you still think your biggest challenge is speaking?"

George stood and replied, "Well, I understand now how important listening is, and how I don't do it very well."

"No, you don't," the woman sitting next to him spoke up playfully.

"Ladies and gentlemen," The Greatest Networker said, obviously amused, "may I introduce you to Mrs. George. Is that correct, ma'am?"

She indicated that it was, and we all had a laugh.

"Well, my dear—what is your name?" he asked.

"Janet," she replied from her seat.

"Janet, we're workin' on that one with George right now. I promise before the lights go out tonight you will have been *heard*. Certainly you'll be listened to more than you were on the drive over here this morning," he said with a broad smile.

"So, George," he said, turning his attention back to the man who was still standing, "you see that you could be a more Creative Listener, less reactive—correct?"

"Yes," he said.

"You got that listening was important, and you saw that there's an opportunity for improvement there for you—yes?"

"Sure," George said.

"Now, George, I got the sense—and I'm not mind-reading here, I'm asking you—I got the sense there was a 'but' coming. Is that true?"

"I'm not sure what you mean," George told him, looking a bit puzzled.

"It sounded as if you were going to say, 'Listening is important,' and you could be better at it, *bu-ut.* . . . But what, George?"

"But I still think I'm not good at speaking."

"Great!" The Greatest Networker said. "George, that's perfect. Thank you for saying that.

"Okay," he said to the group, then turned back to George, "Thanks, George. You can sit down now. The heat's off," he added with a laugh.

"Remember earlier I told you there's a shortcut I can show you which, with practice, could help you become master speakers in a very short time?" he asked, searching our faces.

"Good. Now," and you could sense his growing enthusiasm with what was about to come next, "remember the story of the psychiatrist and the plane flight from New York to L.A.?" Again he looked to the audience.

84

"What did the psychiatrist do?" he asked, and led us to the answer by saying, *"He-e. . . ."*

We finished his sentence just the way he wanted, responding as a group: "Asked questions."

"Great!" he exclaimed. "What bright and charming people—I love Network Marketers!" He clapped his hands with delight.

"Ask questions. That's it! The shortest way to becoming an engaging, empowering, *masterful* speaker, and to *always* be interesting to other people, to get into relationship quickly, meaningfully, successfully—is simply *ask questions*.

"Any questions?" He asked *us* with a laugh.

After a short silence, someone asked back, "How do you begin?"

"Great question!" he said, and laughed one of his booming laughs. "Great! The easiest question to start asking that I've ever come across is this: 'Where do you live?'

"You can ask about anything, really," he told us. "See, the real point isn't in the asking. *It's in your listening.*

"'Where do you live?' is a simple, safe, always easy-to-ask question. For one thing, just about everybody *lives* somewhere—even people we call 'homeless.' And that safety part I spoke of is important. You want the people you're in conversation with to feel relaxed, comfortable, and safe, and asking about where someone lives is usually a pretty nonthreatening question.

"You want to stay away from questions that could send the conversation in a negative direction—especially when you just are starting to be in relationship with someone new. Even if the person you're speaking with is unhappy with where he or she lives for whatever reason, you can easily turn the conversation positive by asking where she or he really *wants* to live, and what would it be like there, what kind of house, neighborhood—do you see?"

And I think most everybody did.

"If I've just met you—on a plane, at a vacation spot, waiting for a bus—I want our first conversation to go well. And I want to be able to continue it, too—the next day, next week, whenever. I'm not going to ask you about anything that could get me in trouble with you.

"I stay away from asking about your job and family right away, because that might be a source of unhappiness for some people. I don't ask about religion, sex, politics, or even what you do for fun. Most people in my experience consider a couple of those subjects too personal, and besides, there's a potential can of worms with each of them I'd rather keep the lid on—for the moment.

"My goal here," he told us pointedly, "is to *get into relationship* with you. That's my agenda—and it's my *only* agenda.

"You see, I know that if I simply get into a relationship with someone new every day . . . if I start just one new relationship *every day*, five days a week, in one year, I will have a thriving Network Marketing organization.

"Let's say I work, what? Forty-four weeks a year—two months off for reasonably good behavior," he smiled. "That's 44 weeks times five days per week with one new relationship each day, which is . . ." he paused, adding aside, "higher math was never my strong point."

"Two-hundred-and-twenty," shouted someone from the audience.

"Thank you!" The Greatest Networker shouted back. "Who says engineers don't get into Network Marketing." And we all laughed.

"Two-hundred-and-twenty people in the year. Two-hundred-and-twenty new relationships. Now, you just know I'm going to have, what—say, 10 percent of those relationships grow into partnerships?" he asked us. "No, probably more. I'm charming and smart enough to have 15 percent of them come in the business with me," he smiled.

"How many's that, my engineering friend?" he asked the voice from before.

"Thirty-three," came the reply, "Not an engineer. Accountant," said the voice.

"Cool," The Greatest Networker responded. "What's your name?" he asked, searching the room.

"Vince," said a thirty-something man in a good-looking suit and tie as he stood up in response.

"Thanks, Vince. Now I've made 220 new relationships in a year—any retail customers there?" he asked, and looked around the room. "And 33 new friendships that have become business partners.

"Given that every successful Network Marketer in the world has built his or her business on the efforts of three to five key leaders in her or his organization, what's the chance that I've got the beginnings of a very successful Networking business going and growing here?"

* * *

"THANKS FOR YOUR help, Vince," The Greatest Networker nodded gratefully. "Are you willing to do something with me here?" Sliding out of his chair, he jumped off the stage and walked towards the man.

"Sure," Vince said.

"Great, thanks again," he said sincerely.

"Okay," he addressed the entire audience. "Vince and I are going to have a conversation. I'm going to ask Vince where he lives. Is that okay with you, Vince?"

"Yes sir," was Vince's reply.

"*Sir*," he repeated, almost as a question. "Army? Navy?" The Greatest Networker inquired.

"Mother," Vince said with a smile.

"Ah yes, I had one of those. Evidently, in at least one way, very much like yours." He smiled, and I had the thought that we were about to get a crash course in the art of *relationshipping*. The man was *good*. I could sense Vince was nervous at first, but I could see that he was already beginning to relax.

"While Vince and I talk—and by the way, this will only take two or three minutes at the most—you will all have some work to do. I want you to practice your Creative Listening. Pay close attention to everything Vince is saying. Don't read anything into it. Use Open Listening. Just focus your listening on exactly what comes out of Vince's mouth— his words, not the chatter inside your own head. What Vince says *is* what he means. Not what you *think* he means. People say what they mean, yet we insist we know better. Crazy, don't you think?" he nodded.

"I want you to really *listen* to Vince's answers to my questions. Hang on his every word—I want you to practice the aspect of Creative Listening that I call Listening By Design. In order to do that, you will simply pay particular attention to something very specific in our conversation. I want you to be on the lookout for Vince's *values*," and he emphasized the word strongly.

"Vince's *values* are those things which are most important to him in his life," he continued. "They are what he cares most about, what he has real passion for, and is committed to in his life.

"I want you to listen *by design* for Vince's values because that's what I say you should be listening for in *every* prospecting conversation.

"Values are the building blocks of people's lives, and because they are, they're vital for each of us to explore, experience, and express. Values are the foundation of all our relationships. Unless you know, respect, and honor another person's values, your relationship won't be genuine. You won't have a chance at developing a friendship, let alone a partnership.

"If you think you have a relationship with someone, but don't know his or her values, your relationship is built on sand. In Network Marketing, you must know a person's values in order to see if there's a fit between the two of you," he told us. "And you may already know this, but I'll repeat it anyway, because it is a profound piece of truth much too important ever to assume: Nobody buys until *you* see through *their* eyes.

"See, in our business, nobody *buys* the company. Nobody really *buys* the products, the comp plan, or the opportunity. They *buy* . . . you! They buy a relationship *with you*. And relationships are *always* built on an exchange of values—shared, appreciated, admired, and above all, *honored* values.

"Do you have a real sense of what I'm saying?" He searched our expressions. "Is there anyone who does not understand what I'm speaking about when I use the word *values?*" he asked with the utmost sincerity.

"Please, do not sit there being confused if you are," he said. "If you're not clear, it's my job today to help you understand. You all understand this business of values?"

Most of the audience nodded and many of us looked around to see if there was someone who wasn't following him.

Evidently, there were either some very shy people here, or we were all right with him.

"Good," he said. "Vince, thanks for your patience. Now, for everyone, let me quickly review what we're going to do. I'm going to have a conversation with Vince; meanwhile, you will be listening attentively and fully *with* your Creative, Open Listening—*without* the distractions of thoughts such as judgment, opinion, agree/disagree, evaluations, assessments, comparisons, impatience, or daydreaming. You'll *Stop, Look, and Listen* for Vince's values. You'll Listen By Design for what's most important to him in his life. Got it?"

We did.

"Great. Vince, come on up here and sit with me—and for the rest of you, do you remember the power of masterful applause? Let's welcome Vince now."

The group exploded with applause—we gave Vince a rousing standing ovation complete with whistles and catcalls and commenting back and forth as we had learned to do. Vince arrived at the stage with his flushed face clearly showing he was embarrassed.

The Greatest Networker shook Vince's hand warmly, one hand on his shoulder and invited him to sit on the edge of the stage with him. (Another smart and subtle move to make Vince comfortable, I thought.) He handed Vince a mike and began, "So, Vince, where do you live?"

Vince took a deep breath and dove right in.

"Out by the university," he said.

"What's it like there?" The Greatest Networker asked. I could literally feel the weight of his focused attention on Vince.

"I like the area," Vince replied, matter-of-factly. "It's close enough to where I work that I can walk on nice days. It's neat and clean. Safe, too. The kids really keep it happening."

"What do you mean 'the kids keep it happening?'" The Greatest Networker asked.

"Well," he said, "it's alive. It's fun. Keeps me young," Vince said and laughed. "There are tennis courts, and I can almost always get a game with somebody. It's a great place to meet people. In the coffee bars, restaurants, and clubs, it's easy to strike up a conversation—the kids are so open. And music, there's always music. New bands, jazz, folk, even great classical stuff over at the auditorium. There's always something to do, something new nearly every night."

The entire time Vince was speaking, The Greatest Networker's eyes were glued to his face. His expression was, well, expression*less*, but you could see he was intently interested in what Vince was saying—and that he was interested *in* Vince.

"You're a pretty active guy, aren't you, Vince?"

"Yeah. I'm single. I like being busy. I like people—meeting new people. Women especially," Vince replied a little shyly.

"And why is *that?*" The Greatest Networker asked with a laugh. He put his hand on Vince's shoulder and said, "I know this is personal, Vince, so don't answer if you don't want to: Are you up for something serious—looking for a long-term relationship or just exploring the native population?"

Vince glanced down for a moment—blushing once again— then answered thoughtfully, "I'd have to say I'm exploring, but . . ." and he took a deep breath, "I just came out of a five-year relationship a number of months ago, and I've gotta say, I really liked being together with someone. I'm afraid my bachelor days are numbered. It's the right time. I am the right guy. I'm just being open to the best right woman in the world showing up."

"The best right woman in the world," The Greatest Networker spoke Vince's words back to him. "That's pretty cool, Vince. So you know what you want—yes?"

"Yes, sir, I do," Vince stated definitively.

"And some pretty high standards, too," The Greatest Networker declared as much as asked.

"Yes, sir. That, too," Vince replied with a laugh. "I guess I want a girl 'just like the girl that married dear old dad,'" and he sang as much as spoke the last words of the old song with a laugh.

"Only younger?" The Greatest Networker asked, and Vince nodded, adding, "And definitely Italian."

"How did I know you would say that," The Greatest Networker said with a laugh.

He extended his hand out for Vince to shake, saying, "We're going to stop here, Vince. You're a pleasure. Thanks for speaking with me, and thanks for your honesty. I really enjoy how clear you are about what you like and want.

"Vince," he continued, "you're someone I'd like to get to know. I have to go now—I have this group of people out there," he said gesturing towards the audience, "that I'm going to talk to this afternoon. Do you have a business card and would you be willing to meet me for lunch, coffee, or dinner sometime—or, hey, you said you played tennis, right?"

"Yeah."

"Any good?"

"Some days."

"Well look, on those *other days*—when you're *off* a bit— I'd love to give you a game," he laughed, and Vince laughed with him. "Would you be up for a couple of sets with a 50-year-old guy who's been playing for about a year and just loves it?"

"No problem," Vince replied. "I'd like that."

"So would I, Vince. So would I. That's exciting. Do you have a card with you? I'm *really glad* I talked to you today, Vince. I'd like us to be friends."

Vince was reaching into his pocket for his business card before The Greatest Networker finished speaking.

"And that, my friends," he said to us, "is how it goes. I *will* see Vince again. Probably a couple of times. You can take that to the bank. I'm guessing Vince is a much better tennis player than I am—but hey. That's one. I also would love to get out more and hear some new music. Left to my own devices, I'll stay home listening to what I already know and love. Vince gives me the possibility of learning something new, get an update on the music my kids are listening to.

That's two. Plus, from his response, I'd say Vince is happy and open to our beginning a relationship with each other. Is that true, Vince?"

"Yes, sir," said the ever-polite Vince.

"That's three, four, ten, and more. And you see," he said leaning forward to us, "I didn't say a *word* about my products. I didn't *mention* my company. I didn't even bring up my incredible opportunity. *I don't have to . . .* because the next time we're together, or time two, or three, or ten, Vince will ask me!

"And what, my friends," he asked us earnestly, with his eyes and arms open wide, "do you imagine will happen *then?*"

* * *

VINCE LEFT THE STAGE and sat down to another terrific round of applause (we were getting *very* good at that). The Greatest Networker then perched in his chair again and said, "I want to make absolutely certain that if you only take one thing away from our meeting today, it's this: *Network Marketing is the relationships business.*

"Look back over my talk just now with Vince; was that a prospecting conversation?" he asked us, raising his hand up high encouraging the audience to respond.

"Yes or no?" he asked the group.

From where I sat, it looked and sounded as though everyone had their hands raised, shouting, "Yes!"

"Oh, you are so teachable and coachable—good for you!" he said smiling.

"As I said before, we live in a relative world. Human beings are connected, related, in relationship," he told the group. "And relationships are reciprocal. Give and take. Tit for tat. You scratch my back, I'll scratch yours.

"I've shown an interest in Vince, and you can bet he's going to show interest in me and mine. Next time, or the next, I'm going to ask Vince what he does for a living. When he's done telling me all about that—because I *really, really listen,* and because I ask all kinds of genuinely curious questions, and because I'm interested in *who* Vince is and *how* Vince is—he's gonna ask me what I do.

"And he will, *I promise you.* He cannot help himself," The Greatest Networker told us.

"As I said, we like people who like us. We're interested in people who are interested in us. We care about people who care about us. We *love* people who *love* us! It's just the way Creation hard-wired human beings to go about *being.*

"And my friends," he spoke to us, leaning forward in his chair, "that's all there is to do today in Network Marketing. One of my mentors was Werner Erhard, the personal and organizational transformation pioneer who founded est. Werner had a great saying: 'All there is to do today is all there is to do today, that's all there is to do today,'" he quoted.

"Well, in Network Marketing, all there is to do today *is* relationships: Make new ones, keep old ones, manage crazy ones, warm up cold ones, fix broken ones. Engage in them. Explore them. Enjoy them. Enrich them. Empower them.

"Every day you choose to go to work, focus your attention on building relationships," he continued. "That's what we do in this business. We speak and listen to create relationships that we grow into friendships, which evolve into partnerships, that we develop and duplicate into a powerful sales organization through leadership. Network Marketing is *relationshipping . . . friendshipping . . . partnershipping . . .* and *leadershipping."*

He leaned back with an expression of—and I wasn't sure if it was real or pretended—surprise. "My word, we really *are* in the distribution business. Shipping and receiving—that's what we do: Relation*shipping*, friend*shipping*, partner*shipping*, leader*shipping*. . . . And then we *receive* checks in the mail."

He laughed another of his booming laughs. "Shipping and receiving. What an industry!"

"More than you wanted to know," he smiled at us after a sip of water.

"Let's go back over my conversation with Vince. What we're going to do now is take a close look at Vince's values. Can you all remember back that far?" he asked with a smile. "What were some of the values you heard Vince speak about?"

A woman in the front row raised her hand. He pointed to her and said, "Yes. Please stand. What's your name?"

"Marijke," the woman replied with an accent I took to be European, but couldn't place precisely.

"Marijke," he said back to her, slowly, drawing her name out *Mah-RY-kah.* "What a beautiful name. Where is it from?" he asked.

"It's Dutch. I'm from Holland," she replied.

He smiled at her. "Marijke, what's a value of Vince's you observed?"

"That he likes sports," she said.

"Really?" he asked, his eyebrows raised in surprise. "And how do you know that?"

"Well," she began, "he said he likes to play tennis at the college."

"That's tennis," he said, "but I don't remember Vince saying anything else about sports—did he?"

"Well, no, but if he likes tennis I'm sure he's into other sports, too," Marijke said.

"Ah, my dear, thanks for doing this one with me." Then he addressed the audience. "Marijke just did something we *all do* and we do it *all the time*. Vince didn't say a word about *sports*. Yes, he spoke about tennis, and Marijke *assumed*," and he stressed the word for impact, "that if Vince likes tennis, he'll be into all sports, too.

"Not necessarily true," he stated. "Vince didn't say that. You've got to understand that in Creative Listening, you can't make up stuff people didn't say and run around thinking and saying it as if it were true. I know that's very *creative* of you, but that's not the kind of creativity I'm after here— okay?" I saw his point. Clearly, there was more to this business of Creative Listening than I first imagined.

"Listen only to what comes out of people's mouths. *That's all!* You can only *hear* what they say anyway. The rest you make up. And if you are busy making stuff up, you are not listening."

"What about non-verbal communication?" a man from the other side of the room stood and asked.

"Yes, yes," The Greatest Networker said to him, "that bit about 90 percent of all communication being non-verbal— right?"

"Exactly," the man replied.

"Well, I don't know about you, my friend, but I have a heck of a time figuring out what most non-verbal communication *means*. I haven't found a copy of the 123rd Edition of Webster's Unabridged Collegiate Non-Verbal Dictionary on Amazon.com yet, either," he said smiling. "Do any of you really understand this non-verbal stuff? Any of you men here today understand the non-verbal communications of the women in your lives?" he asked, as most of the audience laughed.

"You know what this look, that shrug, the head tilted this way means . . . you know what the arms crisscrossed that way from your kids means," and he demonstrated each of these poses in an exaggerated and amusing way. "But do you know what any of these gestures *really* mean?"

He paused for a moment, laughed to himself, and said, "Okay," letting a short but deep breath. "I have to tell you this story. Here goes. . . . This guy was walking on the beach in California," he began. "He looks down and there's this old bottle lying there. He thinks to himself, 'Hey, a genie in a bottle,' and he laughs and walks away up the beach.

"Well, he just couldn't get that darn bottle out of his mind," The Greatest Networker said, and you could tell he was really warming to his story. "So the guy turns around and walks back down the beach, picks up the bottle and pulls out the cork." As he said this, he made a popping sound and jumped off his chair.

"And *whoosh*, all this smoke appears and billows up in a gigantic mushroom cloud and there's thunder and lightning, and sure enough, this genie the size of the Empire State Building leans down and thanks the man profusely for freeing him from 3,000 years of imprisonment in that little bottle. The genie tells him he's going to grant him one wish—just one—and he'd better make it a really good one, 'cause he's only going to get *one wish*.

"It just so happens this guy's a very successful Network Marketer." We all chuckled. "He tells the genie that he's already got most all the material things he's ever wanted—a couple of million dollars, 14,000 square foot house on the beach, boats, all the toys, he travels first class. . . . So he says to the genie, 'You know, I really love to drive, and my MLM company gave me this great S500 Mercedes, and I'd love to drive that car somewhere really fun, somewhere no one has ever driven a car before.'

"'I got it,' the guy says to the genie. 'I want to drive to *Hawaii.*' Well," The Greatest Networker said gesturing dramatically, "the genie rolls his eyes and puts his hands on his head and shakes back and forth saying, '*No, no, no.* Do you have any idea how *hard* that would be? Oh, the engineering, the structural design, the materials it would take to build a road like that across the Pacific Ocean! Please. *Please!* Can't you come up with some other, *easier* wish?'

"The guy, disappointed, thinks for a moment and finally brightens up. He says to the genie, 'Okay, I've got it. I really want to understand my wife's non-verbal communication.'

"And the genie says," he paused, "'Do you want that two lanes or four lanes?'"

The audience erupted in laughter.

The Greatest Networker turned to the man who had spoken and said, "I don't mean to make fun of you—what is your name?"

"Paul," the man replied, still chuckling at the joke.

"Thanks for asking the question, Paul," he said. "I know non-verbal communication exists, and I'm guessing it matters—for men, women, *and* children. However, I don't know for certain what most or any of it honestly means, so I ask questions and listen to the answer because I trust you to tell me the truth. I don't trust my judgment about what your gestures or facial expressions really *mean*. Do you see where I'm going with this, Paul?"

Paul nodded his head in agreement, said 'Yes,' and sat down.

"So, Marijke," he asked, turning back to the woman from Holland, "do you understand what I'm saying about your thought that Vince playing tennis makes sports a value of Vince's?"

"Yes," she answered.

"Now, it *might* be. And the way to know is to ask him. So, Vince," The Greatest Networker turned, "is playing sports a value of yours?"

"Well, actually," Vince replied, standing up as he did, "I'll watch sports on television once in a while, but not as much as I used to. Mostly just the play-offs or Championship games. I just love tennis, that's all," he said. "It's one-on-one. The best man or woman—that day, that match, the one with the skills, the mental composure and control, the one who's the fittest and who wants it the most—wins. I really love that."

"Marijke," The Greatest Networker looked from Vince to her, "do you see?" She nodded her head yes.

"And please, don't feel bad," he said soothingly. "You did what we all do. You were practicing Closed Listening, Listening By Default. You were listening *to you*, not to Vince. And do you know why you did it?" he asked her.

"Because I'm human," she replied.

"*Right!*" he shouted, obviously pleased. "We all do it. Human beings all do it. We make stuff up about what other people are saying and have said. My guess is we hear only 20 percent of what the other person is really saying. The 80 percent we *think* we've heard is stuff we made up. It's not true. It's not even what the person spoke. But we'll swear under oath that it's what he or she said.

"Is it any wonder," he asked us, "that so many marriages don't last? That work doesn't work anymore? That countries don't get along? Is it any wonder," he said, leaning forward, "that so many Network Marketing hopefuls *fail . . .* and fail *so fast?*

"You cannot build a successful business unless you *listen* to people. Remember," and he stood up as he said this, "nobody buys until you see through their eyes, and the *only* way to do that is to *listen!* It's the *only* way!

"*Mah-RY-kah*, my dear," he said, drawing out the woman's name with obvious delight, "did you see any other values when Vince and I talked?"

"Yes," she said matter-of-factly, "he enjoys music and meeting new people."

"Excellent!" The Greatest Networker exclaimed. "That he does. And you know, music and tennis in and of themselves aren't really values. It's what music and tennis *provide* for Vince. It's what he experiences or is able to express *through* tennis, *through* music, even *through* meeting people, which is *of* value to him and therefore one of his values. Vince *gets* something from music. He *gets* something from tennis. And he *gets* something from being with people. It's what he gets that makes up his values.

"You know, that's very interesting." He was silent for a few moments.

"I was just thinking," he said, sitting back down—or up—in his tall chair, "You are *marketers*. That's what you're doing in your full- or part-time career. You are *Network Marketers*. You market to your network of contacts and you build a sales network to market with you and for you. As professional marketers, one thing you must master is the difference between *features* and *benefits*.

"And as every good marketer knows," he said, "features tell, benefits sell. A feature may tell a prospect all about why a given benefit is for real, but it is the *benefit* your prospect is really after.

"A feature," he went on, "is about your product, your company, or you. A benefit is all about *them*. The benefit is the payoff, it's the what's-in-it-for-me your prospect really is interested in getting.

"The often-wrong-but-never-in-doubt, former reclusive marketing genius, Randy Gage, taught me that the way to know if something's a benefit is if it makes sense to put the words *'you get'* in front of it. That tells you there's real value in it.

"For example, take this statement: 'Our company is 15 years old.' Feature or benefit?" he asked the group.

The response from the audience was a mix of both.

"Okay," he said, "just put 'you get' in front of it: '*You get* a 15-year-old company.' What's the benefit?"

Someone from the other side of the room shouted, "You probably get your check on time!"

"*Yes!*" shouted The Greatest Networker in return. "Great! But the fact that you'll get your check on time, every time—who's that about?"

"Me. . . . My prospect. . . . Them. . . ." came the answers from the group.

"So, in a word, the benefit there, the 'you get', is what?"

"Security," a number of people answered.

"Right. Now, you can weave together the benefits supported by features for a pretty compelling presentation. Our company offers you the *security*—there's the benefit—of a proven fifteen-year track record—there's the feature which supports the benefit. How about this—they've *been there and done that* and *increased sales every single month* since they started in business," he said.

"So," he asked, "would you say you have features or benefits in the 'been there, done that' part?"

"Features," a chorus of voices shouted.

"Good. Why?"

"It's all about the company," the man next to me replied.

"Right," The Greatest Networker said, clapping his hands together.

"There's no 'you get,'" a woman in back said.

"Also right. But if we'd said, 'They've never once missed paying out commission checks to their distributors and you can count on them to be here, alive, kicking, and continuing to help you grow your business 20 years from now,' what are the benefits?" he asked.

"Trust," someone said. "A company you can trust."

"Ah, very good," he said. "Anything else?"

"You can count on the company. They're dependable," someone else said from the back of the room.

"Great!" he exclaimed.

"Integrity," another voice said.

"How so?"

"They've paid checks every month," came the response.

"So?"

"Well, they keep their promises. I can count on them."

"Very good!" The Greatest Networker replied, obviously pleased. "Anything else?"

A woman two chairs down from me stood and said, "Obviously the people who run the company really know what they're doing. They're good businesspeople. They've increased sales every month since they started," she said, "which means I've got a powerful business partner I can be proud of who knows how to help me succeed!"

"*Fantastic!*" he said, jumping out of his chair, coming to the front of the stage and pointing to the woman who had just finished. "That's great! You got this business of benefits and features really quickly.

"The real *benefits* of your product and opportunity are *what's important for your prospect.* You learn about them through having a conversation with the person, listening for values, and then pointing out where there's a fit—when, where, and how the products and opportunity will give benefits your prospect wants.

"My point here," he said, returning to his chair, "is that benefits are much like values. In Vince's case, tennis and music are kind of like features which *provide* benefits or values for him. Some of Vince's values that tennis honors—that tennis helps him experience and express—are what?"

I raised my hand, and he called on me immediately.

"Well," I began, hesitantly, "Vince enjoys competition, so I'd say that's a value of his."

"Good," he said, smiling at me. "Go on."

"And he likes to *win*," I told him.

"Yes, he does," The Greatest Networker wholeheartedly agreed.

"And as Marijke said, Vince enjoys meeting people," I told him, "and he said he can almost always find someone to play with and talk to, so I'd say relationships are important to him, too. Now, I'm not sure what values he gets out of relationships, so I'd have to ask him about that.

"But I'd bet," I continued, "Network Marketing would be perfect for Vince, because he can compete, he can win, and perhaps he'd be interested in helping other people win, too."

"Great. That's *really* great," he said approvingly. "Based on that, is there a question you'd ask Vince?"

"Well," I said, "I'd ask Vince if I could show him how he could play a great new business game in which he'd get to win big while all the other people he played with won big, too. I'd ask him if he'd be interested in having a conversation with me about that possibility."

The Greatest Networker just stood there nodding his head and smiling at me.

"So, Vince," he called out, "what's your answer to my friend's invitation?"

"You bet!" Vince exclaimed.

"Thanks," he said to me as I sat down. "That was excellent!"

* * *

"ANYONE ELSE?" The Greatest Networker asked.

A man in back spoke up, "He likes the outdoors."

"How so?"

"Well, he likes to be outside, in nature. He likes to walk to work and play tennis, and that's outdoors."

"Ah ha,' The Greatest Networker replied. "So Vince," he called out, "are you an outdoor guy, a walker, a nature lover?"

Vince stood and said, "Not really. I mean, I don't dislike nature, but I don't go hiking and stuff like that, if that's what you mean."

"But you enjoy walking to work and playing tennis, and those are outdoor activities," The Greatest Networker pointed out.

"I like to walk to work for the exercise and it's easier than hassling with driving through traffic and finding parking."

"So is fitness a value of yours?"

"You bet!" Vince replied.

"And things with a high hassle factor are not?"

"Absolutely not," Vince replied flatly.

"Like, perhaps, calling a week in advance to reserve a court at a specific time, and getting in your car, and driving 15 minutes to play tennis someplace indoors?" he asked.

"Exactly!" Vince said.

The Greatest Networker turned to the man who had spoken and asked, "What's your name?"

"Pat," the man replied.

"So, Pat, let me ask you," The Greatest Networker said, "is nature and being outdoors a value of yours?"

"Yes," Pat said, "it is."

"I thought as much," he said, and turned his attention to the whole group. "What Pat just demonstrated is something else we frequently do. We lay our values on other people. Pat really likes the outdoors and quite innocently, even enthusiastically, he wants us to like the outdoors and nature, too. He likes people who like nature and being outdoors, because they share his values. True, Pat?"

"Sure," Pat said.

"Similarly to what Pat just experienced with Vince, have you ever wanted the business opportunity for someone *more* than they wanted it for themselves?"

Many people in the audience clearly related to that one.

"We do *that* all the time. We're not listening for their values. We're too busy *giving them ours*. We *like it* when other people share our values, and often we take the shortcut and assume they have the very same values we have. Please, *don't do it!*" he emphasized. "That's an example of Listening By Default. Instead, *just listen*. Listen By Design. Discover what *they* want from the business. Find out what values they have that Network Marketing and a relationship with you would honor. That's Creative Listening.

"Pat, thank you. That was a great contribution," The Greatest Networker acknowledged.

"Can you all see how *very* important listening is in Network Marketing?" he asked. My sense was that everyone in the room was clearly getting the message in one way or another.

* * *

"OKAY," The Greatest Networker continued, "so you discovered a number of Vince's values here. And there were others: He likes to do *new* things. As my friend said, he's got a bit of a competitive streak and likes to win. Meeting people is important and relationships are one of his values. So is being busy. He likes things free of hassles.

"Now," he asked us, "are any of those values *valuable* for you to know in learning if there's a fit between you, your Network Marketing opportunity, Vince, and what he wants for his life?" We answered affirmatively.

"Good," he said to us. "Now I want you to turn to the person sitting next to you—left, right, in front of you or behind, any direction is fine—and one of you begin by asking 'Where do you live?' Just like I did with Vince.

"Will five minutes be enough time? Five minutes for each person to ask and answer for a total of ten minutes?"

We agreed.

"Great. I'll tell you when five minutes is up so you can switch who's asking and who's answering. Remember, ask questions, just like I did with Vince. And, oh . . ." he interrupted himself, "let me give you a couple of great questions to help you in this conversation. First one: 'What do you like best about that?'

"That question always moves the conversation in a positive direction. Talking about what they dislike, I say, really doesn't bring out the best in people. In a prospecting conversation, that's what I think you want to know most about—their best," he told us.

"I know some marketing people have the attitude that you should *stir the pain,*" he continued, "find out people's problems, show them how really bad the situation is, then like the proverbial breath of fresh air, provide the solution," he said. I could hear a hint of disdain in his voice.

"That's not what I recommend. More flies with honey," he said. "I'm suggesting that what you really want to talk about is, 'What do you like *best?*' You're after people's values, their dreams, their aspirations, what's most important to them in their lives.

"You might remember that in the last few national elections in the United States, the candidates who won were the ones with the positive advertising, not the mud-slinging, negative ad campaigns. Look at all the upbeat books that offer hope on the bestseller lists—some of them have been there for years. No," he said, "leave the negativity to your competition, and you'll win every time.

"Another very valuable thing to say is to ask the other person simply to tell you more. 'Tell me more about that . . .' or just, 'Tell me more . . .' helps keep the conversation going and going and going. It communicates your interest and caring, which makes people feel comfortable, honored, and respected.

"That question about what they like best, and the request to hear more, will help you in having easy, interesting, and productive conversations in this exercise.

"So," he said to us, "ask, ask, ask! Ask questions for clarity. Make certain you're clear and understand what the other person is saying. Ask for more. Get to their values. A Mercedes isn't a value, but safety, prestige, beauty, status, luxury, comfort, and excellence *are*, so tease out the essence, the values. Find the benefits behind the features.

"Start now, please," he said checking his watch. The room quickly filled with the buzzing of a hundred-plus conversations all beginning with the same question: 'Where do you live?'

Chapter Six
Values, Commitment, and Synergy

W HEN THE FULL ten minutes were up, he called for us to stop, which we did eventually, but only after he clapped his hands together loudly a couple of times and shouted, "Stop now!"

"Okay," he said, "there's another part to this exercise. I want you to get back with your partner again, and this time speak with each other about the values you discovered from your 'Where do you live?' conversation. And there is a best way to do this," he added. "Simply *ask*.

"When you think you've learned one of your partner's values, simply ask him or her, 'Is such-and-such a value of yours?'

"*Please*," he urged, "do not *tell* people what their values are. Most of us grown-ups don't like to be told what to do, and we certainly put up some first-class resistance when other people try to tell us what we're thinking or feeling.

"Is that true for you?" he asked us as a group. We nodded, and some of us agreed aloud.

"Ask your partner if what you *think* you heard to be one of his or her values really is. It would be great to write these values down, because you'll be using them later on today. Okay, ready to begin?

"Great!" he responded to the "Yes!" from the audience. "Begin now. I'll tell you when the time's up."

* * *

WHEN WE'D FINISHED exchanging our values with our partners, The Greatest Networker asked a number of us to stand and share the values we'd found with the group. Some of the values I heard people come up with were freedom, security, intimacy, integrity, adventure, play, fun, humor, belonging, success, recognition, excellence, creativity, relationship, partnership, communication, contribution, wisdom, spirituality, love, and more.

A few people seemed actually surprised at the values they discovered. Everyone was clearly *inspired* by the exercise. That's certainly how I felt. It was an *amazing* experience to be in a room with hundreds of men and women listening to people share the things that were most important for them in their lives. There was a great deal of passion and excitement in that room.

He asked for each of us to take a moment and review our list of values, writing down any more we could think of, prompting us to look at what was really important in all the different areas of our lives: careers, home and family, recreation and play, health, faith, and dreams.

After about two minutes, he went on to say that values exist in being, not in having or doing. That was good news, he told us, because we were, after all, human *beings*, not human *doings* or human *havings*.

He said that when we were experiencing and expressing our values—or honoring another person's values—that's when we were truly and fully *being*.

"Have—have not. Do—do not. So what?" he said, and he added that Shakespeare was right on when he wrote Hamlet's lines: 'To be or not to be? That is the question.' "The *only* question that really matters," The Greatest Networker told us.

I remembered in our previous meetings and conversations—and especially listening to him and standing on stage the other night—how much he focused on being; as when he said that the way you *became* successful was first by *being* successful.

Was it only one week ago? Wow, now that's amazing!

Anyway, I was sitting there, and I had the thought that we—you and I—spend most of our time working on the *having* and the *doing* of our lives. That's what most of the books and tapes are all about: To have this, do that, do this, and have that. But what he was saying was that we shouldn't concentrate our attention on those things.

Everything we wanted to accomplish in life and work, he told us, would come from *how* and *who* we were being. Being was the source, *our* source. All our doing and having—good, bad, or indifferent—came from our being. Be good, be bad, be indifferent, he said, and that's what you will have and do in your life. If you want to know who you have been *being*, he told us, just look at what you do and have in your life right now.

I found all of this "being" stuff very interesting, indeed. Who am I being right now? That was a question *always* worth asking and answering, I thought.

* * *

SOMETHING ELSE THAT really got my attention was what he said about commitment.

He asked every person in the group to consider the question: 'What am I committed to?'

"You are always *living* your commitment," he told us. "You are always *being* what you are truly committed to. You are *unstoppable* in this. Whether we were committed to our problems or our dreams; to avoiding responsibility or achieving success; to taking life easy or making a difference no matter what effort it takes. We are *being* whatever we are committed to. Are you familiar with the quote about commitment from W. H. Murray—one of the men who climbed Mount Everest early on, I think he was in the second expedition—do you know that quote?" he asked, scanning the audience for a sign that we did or didn't.

"Let me read it for you," he said, walking back to the table, opening his tan leather notebook and putting on his pair of small, horizontal reading glasses.

"*Commitment*," he began reading with a reverent tone in a deep radio announcer voice. "*Until one is committed there is always hesitancy, the chance to draw back, always ineffectiveness. Concerning all acts of initiative (and creation), there is one elementary truth, the ignorance of which kills countless ideas and splendid plans: That the moment one definitely commits oneself, then Providence moves, too. All sorts of things occur to help one that would never otherwise have occurred. A whole stream of events issues from the decision, raising in one's favor all manner of unforeseen incidents and meetings and material assistance, which no man could have dreamt would have come his way.*

"I have learned to have great respect for one of Goethe's couplets," he said, taking off his glasses and looking out at us, speaking in a tone of voice that commanded everyone's attention. "He writes, 'Whatever you can do, or dream you can, begin it. Boldness has genius, power, and magic in it.'"

He closed the book and was silent for a short time, letting the meaning and message of what he'd read sink in.

"Would you agree that commitment is required for your success?

"Good," he replied to our show of agreement.

"Do you know that commitment is also required for failure?"

From the looks around the room, this one caught a lot of people by surprise. I hadn't really thought about it that way before.

"How many of you know the name Richard Buckminster Fuller?"

Not many people raised their hands.

"Ah, good. Let me introduce you to him. Buckminster Fuller," he began, "was known as 'the people's genius,' yet he was expelled from Harvard—*twice*—and attended the U.S. Naval Academy at Annapolis without ever completing his formal education! He was a world-renowned architect, engineer, inventor, philosopher, and poet, responsible for the Geodesic Dome, Dymaxion Car, Synergistic Geometry, and the man who coined the term 'Spaceship Earth.' Let me read you a quote of his," he said, reaching for his notebook and putting on his glasses.

"'*For the first time in history,*'" he read, "'*it is now possible to take care of everybody at a higher standard of living than any have ever known. Only ten years ago the more-with-less technology reached the point where this could be done. All humanity now has the option of becoming enduringly successful.*' Buckminster Fuller, 1980.

"Neat, huh? Bucky also spoke about the kinds of people there are in the world," he told us. "And this is another thing I learned from my friend and mentor Carol McCall. There are people who are asleep; people who are stirring—caught between sleeping and waking; people who have just awakened; and people who are wide awake.

"As I describe these kinds of people to you," The Greatest Networker said, "think of the men and women you've prospected for your business, and see if you recognize this description of any of them.

"Tell me, have you ever encountered someone who is sound asleep? When you talk to them, what happens?

"Right, nothing. They're asleep!" he said, answering and playing with the phrase. "Even if you did wake them up to share with them the most profound truth you'd ever heard, they'd go right back to sleep. Why? Because that's what they're committed to—*being asleep!*

"Have you ever met anybody who was like that—yes, they're walking around, but they're sound asleep. Have you ever talked with a prospect who was like that?" Many of us in the audience laughed.

"Now, here's the really funny part: How often are we telling these sleeping people all about our opportunity—*the greatest opportunity in the history of the world*—and wondering *why* they don't *get it?*

"They're asleep!" he exclaimed. "That's why! Yet we keep talking and talking to them. How about those people who are between sleeping and waking? How do they respond?" he asked.

"*They don't,*" he answered. "They can't. They're not awake yet. They're not even sure if waking up is what they want to do. Most of them aren't committed to waking up— they're more interested in hitting that snooze-alarm to get another five minutes of shut-eye."

It was clear he was having fun with this, and I knew most of the people in the audience were getting the message behind the humor.

"Those folks who've just awakened," he continued, "are they ready to answer your questions? What do you think will happen when you go up to someone who's just awakened from a sound slumber, sitting up rubbing the sleep from his eyes, and you come along and say, 'Hi there. Where do you live?'" And he laughed as he said this.

"My friends, the only people you want to be speaking with are the ones who are *wide awake*. Those are the people with 'ears to hear.' They are the men and women who are committed to being awake in life. They're looking. They're listening. They're ready to pay attention to what you have to share. With all the others, you are wasting your time and theirs.

"Please, don't fight the city hall of what people are committed to," he cautioned us. "Let the people who are asleep sleep. Let the people who are just waking up or who just woke up alone. Let them be, because who they are *being* is someone who isn't awake yet.

"*Are you awake?*" he shouted.

"*Yes!*" we roared back.

"Good. I know that. You wouldn't be spending your Saturday here with me if you weren't. All of you are men and women with a commitment to learning, to growing and developing, and to being more successful today than you were yesterday. I'll bet you know some people in your organization who are not here today—yes?" he asked.

Many people nodded agreement or said "Yes."

"Simply put, they're committed to something else today," he said. "Cartoons, maybe. Or mowing the lawn, or going shopping. And *that's fine*. That's fine. Lawns need mowing, cartoons need watching, and, when the going gets tough, the tough go shopping," he added with a laugh.

"It's always about what you commit to. That's why the question 'What are you committed to?' is so important. In any situation, you can always Stop, Look, and Listen. Stop: Ask yourself what you're committed to. Look and see, and Listen. Listen to the answer. If what you are committed to does not empower you, change your mind and commit to something that does.

"Yes, you can always change your mind. We do it all the time. Put a thought in your mind right now," he said impulsively. "Any thought will do, just think of something, anything.

"Now," and he snapped his fingers loudly, "change your mind. Have another thought right now!

"Perfect," he said, snapping his fingers again. "Now, make another, different thought."

Snap! "And another one, now!"

Smiling, he told us, "Look, it may take some of you a little more practice, but I'll bet most of you are really good at changing your mind already. Is that true?" All of us in the audience raised our hands in quick response.

"Great," he said, settling back into his chair. "Oh, you know . . . well, you probably don't know," he kidded himself. "There's another of Bucky Fuller's quotes I love. Check *this* one out: 'Sometimes I think we're alone. Sometimes I think we're not. In either case, the thought is staggering.' Isn't that *good!*"

I hadn't heard that one before. I smiled and wholeheartedly agreed with him: It was *really* good.

"I know I'm jumping around here today," he added thoughtfully. "Running down a number of different tracks at the same time, but speaking about Buckminster Fuller reminded me of something I want to tell you about. So, yet another track to run on," he laughed.

"How many of you are familiar with the term *synergy?*"

A small number of people scattered throughout the audience raised their hands. I had known about Fuller and his geodesic domes and synergy from my early days back with computers at MIT, and I'm always surprised at how few people know about Bucky's ideas. He was one of the most original and creative thinkers America's ever produced. Although he's been dead for a number of years, I think he still is—a most original and creative thinker, I mean.

"Synergy," he told the group, spelling the word out, S - Y - N - E - R - G - Y. It's when the whole is greater than the sum of its individual parts. One reason synergy is important for Network Marketers to understand and appreciate is that while most other business systems develop by addition or multiplication, ours grows geometrically, exponentially by synergy.

"Now, you may have seen or heard about an over-matched team that won the big game, beating a team that had much greater talent or far more experience," he said, "like the U.S. Hockey Team that won the gold medal in the Olympics by beating the vastly superior Russian players. There are many examples from sports, business, the military, all aspects of life. Well, Fuller created a formula to calculate the effect of synergy," he said.

"It's really simple. Let's take all the people in this room here today for example. There are, what, 250? That's the number of people here, but that's not all there is here in this room today. There are a number of *relationships* here, too. And *that* number," he emphasized, "may surprise you. Bucky's formula is as follows: P squared, minus P, divided by two, equals the amount of S, which stands for Synergy—okay?"

I wrote the equation down on my notepad . . .

$$\frac{P^2 - P}{2} = S$$

. . . as he explained, "Take the number of people present—the 250 people here today, and square it—the number of people times the number of people. That's 250 x 250 . . . Vince, have you got the answer?" he called out.

"62,500," Vince shouted back.

"Vince, you're terrific," The Greatest Networker said. "Are you just as good with tax savings and deductions?"

"Better!" came Vince's to-be-expected reply.

"Great! I'll call you Monday. So, 62,500 minus 250 is. . . . It's okay, Vince, I can do this one myself," he laughed. "That's 62,250. Divided by two equals. . . ." He thought for a moment and just before he spoke, an attractive woman with long dark hair in the first row on the other side of the room shouted the answer, "31,125."

"Thank you, my dear," he said, looking over at her. "Are you Italian?"

She replied by nodding silently with a big wide smile, and The Greatest Networker quipped suggestively, "Have you met *Vince?*" Everyone in the room laughed. I imagined Vince was blushing, although I couldn't see him from where I sat.

"I'd be happy to introduce you," he said. "Do you play tennis, by any chance? Okay, okay," he said, putting up his hand to quiet our laughter and get himself back on track, "31,125 is the synergistic answer, but what does that really mean? What's the significance—*the benefit*—of that number for each of you?"

He looked around for a moment, and since nobody volunteered—and I'm certain he didn't expect anyone to—he continued, "It means that in this room of only 250 people there are actually *31,125 relationships!*

"You and I," he pointed to one person, then to another, "and you and I, and you and I," he began referring directly to each of the people he had pointed to in the audience, "and you and you and you and you . . . and you and you. This may be confusing for some of you at the moment, but relax, it will all be crystal clear very soon, I promise.

"You see," he continued, jumping down off the stage to make his illustration clear. "You and I are one relationship," he said, pointing to the first person he'd selected. Then, turning to the next person, he said, "And you and I are one relationship. And you and you," he said, pointing to both of those people he'd picked out, "are one relationship. So, there are three of us and we have three relationships between us— can you all see that?" he asked the group.

"Now, the fun part. Let's add you, sir." He selected a tall man in front, then added, "Would the three of you stand here so the people in the room can get this visually?"

The three people stood up and he had them move to the stage and turn around to face the audience.

"Thanks," he told them, and then he said to the man he asked to stand last, "Now, we had three of us and there were three relationships between us before we asked you to join— right? Has everybody got that so far? Me to you, and me to you, and the both of you to each other—three," he said, pointing to the first two people and himself.

"Then you joined us, my friend," he said putting his hand on the man's shoulder. "How many relationships are there now with all of us up here? Let's count them.

"You and I—that's one. Me and this lady—that's two. Me and this gentleman—that's three. Those two with each other—that's four. And you," he said pointing to the tall man and then to the woman, "with this lady is *five*, and you and this gentleman is . . . *six!*" he said with mock surprise.

He stood apart from the three people in the front of the room and said, "Isn't *that* interesting. When there were just three of us, we had three relationships, but when this gentleman joined us, we all of a sudden had *six* relationships between us.

"That, my friends," he announced to the entire room, "is *synergy*. There are more relationships here amongst our little group than there are people! And every time we add another person, the number of people grows by one, but the synergy, the number of relationships we share together, *grows exponentially!*" he said with great emphasis.

"Just do the math. Four people together—six synergistic relationships. Add one, five people together—how many is that?" he asked, and before we could answer he called out laughing, "Vince, you and your fiancée stay out of this! With five people . . ." and he quickly asked someone in the first row to stand and join the group up front, "how many synergistic relationships? Do the visual," he said, pointing back and forth to each person counting the relationships.

"No, that's too confusing," he said shaking his head. "Let's do the math equation instead. Use Bucky's formula. Five squared is 25, minus five is 20, divided by two equals ten—there are ten relationships here now.

"Let's add another person," and he had someone else go up and join the group. "Now we are six," he said, "and 'we're clever as clever and we hope we'll be six for ever and ever.'"

Some of us who knew the poem laughed at his quick literary humor. He said, "Thanks to all you Winnie the Pooh parents and fans of A. A. Milne. Okay—we are six. How much synergy?"

"Fifteen," someone shouted.

"Right," he exclaimed, "and when we're seven, we'll have 21. And when we are eight, there will be 28. Nine is 36. Ten is 45, 11 is 55, 12 is 66. Do you see the way these numbers are *growing?*" he asked excitedly.

"They are growing *geometrically!*" he exclaimed. "Synergy is *ex - po - nen - tial*. This is how your Network Marketing organization grows. This illustration of synergy gives you an actual look at the size and shape and growth of your future!

"And the fascinating part," he added dramatically, "the amazing thing . . . is that all you do is add one person at a time—*just one person at a time!* That's how you build a huge organization! That's how you get a monster check in the mail! That's how you make a difference in thousands, even millions of people's lives!

"*Just one person—one relationship—at a time*," he said, and looked at us all in silence.

* * *

AFTER HE THANKED all the people he had brought up front, asking their names, thanking them personally, and telling each that he appreciated them, he asked us to acknowledge them all. We responded with a masterful storm of 'thunder and lightning' applause, and he took his seat on the front edge of the stage.

"Wow," he said, "we've covered a lot of territory this morning. *Too* much I think," he said, which was greeted by shouts of "No, no!" and "More! We want more!"

"Thanks," he smiled, returning the acknowledgment. "I appreciate you, too."

He took a deep breath, went over to the table beside his chair and reached for a bottle of water. After taking a long drink, he sat back down again on the stage.

He exhaled deeply and quickly. "What I want to do next is give you a shot at getting in touch with your Life Purpose. And I know you've been in here a long time and you're probably hungry. . . ." He scanned the audience and got his answer. "Yes, you want to take a break and eat. I understand.

"Okay, it's your choice," he announced. "We can cover this part with a demonstration in, say . . ." he looked at the watch on his outstretched wrist, "ten minutes or so, then break for lunch and have you guys do some work with each other, or we can stop now, do the Life Purpose segment after lunch as a group, and finish up my part of the afternoon. What would you like?"

"Which is best?" someone shouted.

"They both are," The Greatest Networker replied. "Are you asking which I think you should choose?"

"Yes," came a chorus of responses.

"Well," he said with a laugh, "I never eat lunch, so I'm the wrong guy to ask. But if I were you, I'd vote for lunch now, without homework, 'cause we covered a lot of ground this morning, and I'm guessing some of you would like to rest your minds.

"Now!" he exclaimed and stood up. "That does not mean you don't have to *listen*. And believe me, listening is sometimes *very* hard work. So my assignment for you over lunch is, no matter what conversation you're involved in, practice asking questions and listening. Do you agree to my request?"

His question was greeted with a loud and unanimous, "Yes!"

"Good. Go eat. Relax. Meet somebody new, *please!* Sit next to someone you don't know or sleep with," he laughed. "Ask them where they live and come back in an hour and a half, ready to discover your Life Purpose.

"Thank you all," he called out. "I appreciate you." He unclipped his mike, set it on the stage, and left the room.

CHAPTER SEVEN
A "Free-ing" Lunch

WE MOVED AS a group into the room right next door where lunch was being served. Well, not "served" actually; we helped *ourselves* to one of the lushest buffets I'd ever seen.

There were big bowls of assorted greens and platters of fresh vegetables, perhaps half a dozen cold dishes like pasta salads and bean salads with all kinds of sandwich breads and rolls, cheeses, and cold cuts, too.

Given this morning's message about taking care of my body—what did he say, "Whether you consider your body a temple or a tool . . ."—I'd already made the commitment to pass on the desserts and stick with the healthy stuff, or "rabbit food," as my wife, Kathy, would have called it.

I piled my plate high with a variety of salads, but as I walked on by all those honeyed pastries and chocolate confections, I had the thought that commitment is sometimes *very* difficult indeed.

I paused for a moment and glanced back over my shoulder at the array of rich, delicious desserts. The longing expression on my face must have been funny to see, for a woman I'd been sitting next to in the meeting grabbed my arm as she was walking past and guided me to a nearby table saying, "Get thee behind me, devil's food."

"You must be one of those unforeseen incidents, meetings, and material assistance I've heard tell about," I kidded her.

"Ah, commitment," she quipped and, glancing backward, remarked, "Hard work around *that* dessert table."

"*Very*," I replied.

As luck would have it, my friend directed me to the table where The Greatest Networker was sitting and speaking with a small group of people. He stood up as we reached the table. A gentleman, too, I thought.

"May we join you?" my woman friend asked.

"Please," he said, pulling out the chair next to him for her.

"Your mother must have been quite a lady," she said as she sat down with a smile.

"How so?" he asked.

"You stand up and pull out a chair for a woman. In this day and age, that's remarkable—so I remarked on it. A lost art, I think. And," she added, "when you and Vince were speaking this morning, you commented on his use of the word 'Sir,' and said your mother and Vince's were similar in that regard—they taught you both to be polite."

"I love it when people *listen creatively*," he said, laughing to all of us as he sat down.

"Thank you," he said. "Courtesy is a value of mine, and so is being a gentleman. It makes me feel good. How does that kind of attention make *you* feel?"

"*Wonderful*," she said, placing her hand just below her neck and bowing slightly towards him. "And quite ladylike."

"Ah, good," he smiled.

"You're not eating, or may I get you a plate?" she asked him, noticing the empty space in front of him.

"No, thank you. I'm not all that big on lunch, or breakfast for that matter. I know that's not recommended healthy behavior, but eating during the day always slows me down. So thank you, but I'll just have some iced tea for now."

"May I ask you a question?" the woman who saved me from an attack of *chocoholism* asked.

"Please," he said. "But first, tell me your name."

"Nancy," she said.

He smiled at her, waiting for her question.

"I'm certain you've been asked this many times before," she began, "but I'm curious how you began in this business. What did you do first?"

He smiled his biggest grin and then said, straight-faced, "The first thing I did, Nancy, was *fail*."

He met the puzzled looks on all our faces with one of his booming laughs.

"Truly, I flat-out failed," he said, still chuckling.

"Tell me more," Nancy requested with a wink.

"You could have simply asked me where I lived," he shot back playfully.

A couple joined us at the table, filling the remaining seats. He stood, and so did I. The other two guys were evidently slow learners, I thought at first. Or perhaps being a gentleman just wasn't one of their values. *That* was a much *better* thought—I decided. The Greatest Networker extended his hand, the new people made their introductions, and he presented all of us at the table by name.

When he sat down, Nancy continued. "Please," she said with genuine sincerity, "I'm really very interested in how you started out in this business—what happened and what you did. Will you say more than simply you began by failing?"

"Sure," he said, "I started with the products as a retail customer."

He looked at each of us as he spoke. Just like all the others at the table, I quickly found myself hanging on every word.

"Rachel and I lived by the ocean in New England," he told us. "We had moved out of the city—we'd both lived in cities for years—because I had this radical idea that you can either *take* your vacation or *live* your vacation. Well, I wanted to live it, so we found a great place on the beach. Rebecca, my daughter, was born in the bedroom of that house.

"Anyway, since we were the ones with the house on the beach, all our friends came down to visit us, so even in winter the house was usually full on weekends with visitors and friends coming and going in and out of town.

"Have you ever heard of Macrobiotics?" he asked, searching the faces of the group at the table.

"Yeah," one of the men said, "wasn't that some kind of hippie diet where all you ate was brown rice or something?"

"Close," The Greatest Networker laughed. "There was a lot more to it than just brown rice—and there was a great

130

deal of philosophical study involved as well. In terms of diet, Macrobiotic people ate organically-grown foods, stayed away from over-refined products like white sugar, frozen, canned, and processed foods, artificial additives and the like, didn't eat red meat, mostly fish and tofu for protein. Lots of Japanese foods, too, like soy sauce, miso, umeboshi plums, seaweeds. . . ."

Ah, that explains it, I thought, remembering our dinner at Hiroshi's.

"All in all, when done well, with understanding and flexibility, it was, and in my opinion *still is*, the very best way to eat in the world. The problem was," he explained, "most people didn't do it that way at all.

"You see, the kind of people who were attracted to Macrobiotics were usually those who wanted to cure themselves of some disease or condition using something other than conventional Western medicine—you know, hospitals and drugs. There were a lot of sick people involved back then, and they tended to be pretty rigid about their approach to their diet and lifestyle.

"Fact is," he told us, "most of the people involved looked like they haunted houses for a living." Every one of us around the table had a good laugh at that, especially The Greatest Networker.

"Two of our friends became a couple and decided to run off to the West Coast and see how the other half lived and worked. New England tends to run narrow and deep while California is shallow and wide—these two Yankees set out for San Diego to seek their opposite where there is no winter and it never, ever rains, or so they'd been told.

"Now," he leaned forward and pointed his finger, "they were card-carrying house-haunters these two. They had ashen faces—he was as thin as a rail—and just enough of a lifeless, vacant look in both their eyes to frighten young children and puppies," he laughed.

"About eight months later, we got a call from them: 'Hey, we're making a swing back through town to see old friends this summer and we'd like to stop and stay for a couple of days—okay?'

"'Great,' we told them, and waited for their arrival. When these two characters finally show up, we see that they are *transformed*. I mean, they look *fantastic!* She's glowing and beautiful with rosy cheeks. He looks full and fit and strong, and he's all smiles and lightness and fun.

"Rachel and I ask, 'What *are* you guys doing? You look *incredible*. So healthy, so happy—*what happened?'*

"The answer was . . ." and he paused obviously for effect, "*primordial pond scum*. That's a *technical* term for blue-green algae. 'That's what did it,' they told us, 'we just eat this.'" He held out his hand with the palm up showing us some imaginary somethings like Jack and the Beanstalk's magic beans.

"'*We want some,'* we said. He closed his hand, pulling it back with a smile. "And that was that; we started on the products. Frankly, both my wife and I didn't feel a whole lot different in the beginning, but hey, look what it had done for our friends, so we kept taking it.

"About three weeks after we started eating the algae, we simply forgot to take it for a couple of days. Then about 2:30 one afternoon, Rachel and I turned to each other at the same time and both said we were thinking of lying down—taking a nap. We never did *that*. *Never!*

"We both had the very same thought," he said, with a look of feigned surprise on his face, "*It's the algae!* That crazy primordial pond scum really *did* give us more energy and really *did* make a difference in how we felt. We just had to stop taking it to realize how good we'd really been feeling.

"And that," he told us, sitting back in his chair, "was more than a dozen years ago, and I still take the product. Rachel and I were convinced the product was great and people would really benefit from taking it. Since I was already in the natural food business as a marketing consultant whose job it was to promote healthful food products, since I had a pretty strong circle of influence, *and* since I'd developed a favorable impression of Network Marketing, and mostly because Rachel thought we should give the business a try. . . ."

"Excuse me," Nancy interrupted, "would you say more about your 'favorable impression of Network Marketing?'"

"Sure," he replied, "is there something specific you want to know?"

"No, I'm just interested in what you thought about it."

"Okay. There were many reasons I liked Network Marketing. So, just off the top of my head . . . I saw the business first as a marketer. Nothing will ever be as powerful promoting a product or service as simple word-of-mouth, and Network Marketing harnessed that by giving it a reward structure. I thought that was utterly brilliant!" he said, with obvious admiration.

He took a deep breath. "Person-to-person or relationship marketing is absolutely the *only* way to go. It's the one best way to cut through the absurd amount of ad pollution and excess communication and get past the natural and nearly insurmountable defenses people today have built up against communication overwhelm just to preserve their *sanctity* and *sanity*.

"Look," he said, leaning forward in earnest, "you and I, because we are human beings—especially *American* human beings—are genuinely curious about new products that will enrich our lives. We are, after all, the greatest consumers in the world! We really *want* to know what's new, what's different, and what will make our lives better. But where do we go? Who do we ask?"

"The Internet," one of the men across the table chimed in.

"Very good, Bob," The Greatest Networker said, nodding his head in agreement. "That brings up another great reason Network Marketing has such an extraordinary future ahead. It's not really the answer to Nancy's question, but I think it's fascinating. Do you want to hear about that?" he asked, turning to Nancy.

"Absolutely," she said.

"Cool," he said, "I spent a number of years, decades actually, studying philosophy and comparative religion. Are you all familiar with the Eastern terms, *yin* and *yang?*"

Everybody nodded or said they were.

"Great!" he exclaimed. "They're the two fundamental forces of life—the original opposite poles of the magnet of all Creation. The two energies that bring about day and night, male and female, up and down, action and rest, expansion and contraction. Part of understanding yin and yang—and

134

life itself—is that all Creation operates with universal laws. Go with them and you've got harmony. Forget them, fight them, or challenge them and you'll struggle. The result is discord, difficulty, disease, even death.

"One of these laws is: 'The bigger the front, the bigger the back.' What that means in practical terms is that everything in our universe is relative, everything exists in *relationship* to something else. A change on one side will require a change in the other. Do you understand, or is this too far-out for a Saturday lunch conversation?" he asked us.

I looked around the table, nobody moved. They urged him to please go on. I sat there in amazement, expecting from experience that it would continue. I don't think I'd ever met anyone who knew so much from so many different sources.

As if to prove my point, The Greatest Networker asked the table, "Are any of you familiar with the author Ursula LeGuin?" No one at the table seemed to know her.

"Ah," he said, then asked, "You know Tolkien's *Lord of the Rings* and *The Hobbit* or C. S. Lewis or William Morris— the genre of literature called high fantasy?"

I knew *The Hobbit*, and the others at the table nodded their recognition of some of the other names that he mentioned.

"Ursula LeGuin wrote the Earthsea Trilogy, which is a classic fantasy novel series. I have a favorite passage from *The Farthest Shore*, which eloquently explains this front and back, relative world idea. And hang on," he added with a grin, "this will all connect back to Bob's point."

He leaned forward on his elbows pressing his fingers above his eyebrows as if massaging his mind. Then he looked up and smiled. "Got it," he said, and began to quote the book he'd referred to in that deep, resonant voice of his.

"*Presently the mage said, speaking softly, 'Do you see, Arren, how an act is not, as young men think, like a rock that one picks up and throws, and it hits or misses, and that's the end of it. When that rock is lifted, the earth is lighter; the hand that bears it heavier. When it is thrown, the circuits of the stars respond, and where it strikes or falls the universe is changed. On every act the balance of the whole depends. The winds and seas, the powers of water and earth and light, all that these do, and all that the beasts and green things do, is well done, and rightly done. All these act within the Equilibrium. From the hurricane and the great whale's sounding to the fall of a dry leaf and the gnat's flight, all they do is done within the balance of the whole.'*"

He looked from one to the other of us as he spoke. Then he stopped and smiled, saying, "And this next part—this is so wonderful. '*But we, insofar as we have power over the world and over one another, we must learn to do what the leaf and the whale and the wind do of their own nature. We must learn to keep the balance. Having intelligence, we must not act in ignorance. Having choice, we must not act without responsibility.'*"

He led the group in sitting silently, each one of us considering what we had just listened to in our own way.

"So, Bob," he said breaking the quiet, "you mentioned the Internet and that it's one way you learn about new things. I brought up that remark about the bigger the front, the bigger the back. What I was speaking about—and how I tie all of this back into Network Marketing—is that the more high tech we get, the more high touch we will become as well. It's simply balance within the Equilibrium.

"Every 18 months," he continued, "the capacity and power of the microchip *doubles!* Bob, neither you nor I really have a clue what life—and especially *work*—will be like five or ten years from now."

And Bob nodded his agreement.

"Just look back over what's changed in the last decade alone. The impact of microtechnology on our world is astonishing, isn't it?

"But two things will never change, Bob," he said, leaning over the table in Bob's direction with that intense, focused attention of his, "creativity and relationships. No matter how many billions of pieces of information per nanosecond those microchipsters can process, they will never master the creative feeling-awareness of a human being, and they will never ever take the place of the intimacy of human relationships.

"Creativity and relationships. That means, if you can think and dream, Bob, and you know how to listen creatively, to love and be loved," and he laughed as he added, "'then yours is the Earth and everything that's in it. And—which is more—you'll be a man, my son!'"

"Kipling?" Nancy asked.

"Kipling," he answered.

"Anyway," he said with a deep breath, "the more technology increases its influence in our lives and how we work and what we do, the greater importance will be placed on *relationships*. And since Network Marketing is all about relationships, the demand for our way of doing business will only grow.

"The only better time than today to be involved in Network Marketing," The Greatest Networker told our group at the table matter-of-factly, "is tomorrow. And my guess," he added, "is that the day after that will be even better."

* * *

FROM PRIMORDIAL POND SCUM, to ad pollution in our over-communicated society, to yin and yang, to Ursula LeGuin explaining the—what was it called?—Equilibrium, to microtechnology and high tech creating a lasting future for high-touch Network Marketing, with a dash of Rudyard Kipling . . . *whew!* And we weren't even halfway through lunch yet. *Amazing!*

The Greatest Networker turned back to Nancy and explained more of his "high opinion," as he called it, of Network Marketing—adding with a laugh that he had a high opinion of his opinion.

He told her that in all he had seen of business, Network Marketing was the most fair in terms of responsibility and reward. In our business, he pointed out, you get paid for your productivity and leadership—no more, no less.

He spoke about time and money leverage and residual income, and how Network Marketing opened up—for average people—the possibility of earning money in ways that were once reserved only for gifted artists, inventors, or the wealthy.

He talked about the freedom Network Marketing offered, telling us that he felt extremely fortunate to have worked for himself for years before he got into this business, when most people didn't have that choice. Network Marketing gave it to them, he pointed out.

"Working where, when, and how much *you* want, rather than having your *boss* or some company policy tell you what to do," he told us, "is truly the American way. After all," he added with a laugh, "didn't the 'Declaration of Independent Contractors' say that we Network Marketers are endowed by our Creator with certain inalienable Rights, among which were Life, Liberty, and the Pursuit of Happiness?"

We happily agreed.

"Will you tell me what you meant before when you said you failed?" Nancy asked.

"Sure," The Greatest Networker said. "I was a marketer in the natural foods business; good at it, well known and respected—and well known as someone who only worked for the best companies with the best reputations who made the very best products, too. Best is one of my values," he smiled.

"I was your classic center of influence. That's the good news. The bad news is I was a professional who wrote advertising copy that sold people products, and I was very good at it."

"Why is that bad news?" Rob, one of the men at the table, asked.

"Because it's not—and I wasn't—duplicatable. I decided to write a sales letter for my products. That's what I knew how to do best. I had what we used to call back in the dark ages a desktop publisher. Big 19-inch screen, Xerox computer with eight-inch floppy disks—remember those? Laser printer and all. As I said, I'd been writing advertising copy for a living for years, so I worked-up a killer six-page sales letter and sent it out to all the 165 people on my names list.

"Well, 132 of them responded and bought products from me at retail. Within the first two months, a little over 30 of them signed up as distributors, too. This was back in the days when there were no special sign-up bonuses and extra inducements. It was straight—buy your first order retail, hear the opportunity pitch, sign the application, pay your fee, and be prepared to get rich slow."

"That's impressive success pretty fast," one of the women said.

"Yes, it was," he admitted.

"So how did you *fail?*" Nancy still wanted to know.

"Well by the third month, the only real business I had was a bunch of retail people who had gotten tremendous results and health benefits and some who became wholesale consumers and were reordering products. None of my distributors did a thing in terms of building a business!

"And why should they?" he asked. "How could they? I was a professional marketer. None of them had those skills. I had a huge, decade-old center of influence, and most of them didn't have that either. Besides, I didn't know how to teach anybody how to do the business, because *I didn't have a clue!* All I knew how to do was write a great sales letter and have people respond, but my people couldn't do that.

"That's when I learned my first and most fundamental lesson in this business," he said. "If other people cannot do what you do—*don't do it!* If it's not duplicatable, it's just not Network Marketing."

"So, what's duplicatable?" Randolph, another of the men at the table, asked.

"Randolph," The Greatest Networker replied thoughtfully, "I think the only things worth duplicating are those personal and professional growth skills which contribute to making and keeping relationships, friendships, partnerships, and developing leadership."

"What about having a duplicatable system?" Randolph asked.

"Such as?" The Greatest Networker asked.

"Well, say first you send out a cassette tape to pre-qualify prospects, then a phone follow-up, an info pack, then a step-by-step interview or presentation, then a training."

"Is that what you do, Randolph?"

"No."

"Ah. Randolph, two things: First, the most duplicatable system I know of is Use, Recommend, and Sponsor—*use* the products, *recommend* them to others, and *sponsor* people who'd like to create a Networking business of their own.

"The other point I want to make was taught to me by Russ DeVan—you might remember my mentioning that Russ was the person who taught me how to applaud masterfully." Randolph nodded that he did.

"Russ taught me that all you ever do in Network Marketing is learn how to do a thing and then, once you've become really proficient at that, once you can do it again two, three, five more times yourself, you teach others how to do it, too. In Network Marketing," The Greatest Networker explained, "all you do is teach people how to do what you already know how to do. Is that clear, Randolph? Or would you like an illustration of how that works?"

"It's clear," Randolph said.

Nancy chimed in immediately, "I'd like the illustration."

"Me, too," said Bob.

"Okay," The Greatest Networker began. "You all use your company's products—yes?" The people at the table all said they did.

"Great. Are you competent enough using those products yourself to teach other people how to do that as successfully as you do?"

"Sure. Yes. Of course . . ." we said.

"*Great*," he said again. "Next, you go and find two people—friends, family, people you know right now on a first name basis—who you think or feel would like to get the same positive benefits from using the products that you've gotten." He paused to look around the table, making sure we all were with him. We were.

"You find these two people and you recommend the products to them. You teach them how to do what you already know how to do—*use* the products. Can you do that?"

Everyone at the table replied that they could.

"Good," he said, and leaned forward gesturing with his hands out in front of him. "So now you've got a good little business going. You've got yourself as a customer and two other people who are retail customers of yours.

"Next, you go find two other people and sponsor them. These are people who, just like you, want to build a Network Marketing business. Once again, this is something you already know how to do—you already know how to be a person who wants to build their own business—right?"

"So you find these two people and you teach them how to use the products like you already know how to do. You teach them how to have two retail customers—as you already know how to do. That's sponsoring. Are you with me?" he asked.

"Now look at what you've got: You have two distributors and each of them has two retail customers. And that, my friends," he said, sitting back and spreading his arms wide, "is what we call a Network Marketing *organization*.

"Let's say" he continued, "you and both your retail customers are each purchasing $100 worth of products each month at your wholesale cost. What's the monthly dollar volume for your entire organization?"

"$900," Nancy said quickly.

"Great," he replied. "You already know how to have two distributors who have two retail customers, and a total monthly wholesale volume of $900. You teach your two distributors how to do what you already know how to do: How to sponsor two distributors of their own; each using the products themselves; each recommending the products; having two retail customers; and everybody purchasing $100 worth at wholesale every month.

"Now what do you have?" he asked, and added, "Nancy, you seem to have a calculator mind, what's that amount to?"

"$2,100," Nancy said smartly, smiling, "My $300 and $900 for each of my two distributors."

"Perfect!" The Greatest Networker said, smiling back at her. "What happens next, Nancy?"

"I have a $2,100 monthly volume with two front line distributors who each have two distributors on their front line,"

Nancy said. "So I teach my two how to do what I've done and build their organizations with $2,100 volume for their two distributors down two levels."

"Exactly!" he exclaimed. "And so it goes. Now you've got 14 people in your organization, plus yourself, and a $4,500 volume. Next, you'll have. . ." and he let the question linger in the air, presumably for Nancy to answer, which of course she did immediately.

"$9,300 with an organization of 30 people, plus me," she said with a smile, adding, "and next would be . . . $18,600 plus my volume—$19,000!"

"And - that's - the - way - your - network - grows," The Greatest Networker said, as if speaking a child's nursery rhyme. "And all the time, all you do—all anybody *ever* has to do—is learn how to do something, become competent at it, and then teach others how to do what they already know how to do.

"Use, recommend, sponsor, and teach people how to do what you already know how to do.

"Randolph," he said turning to the man, "that's a duplicatable system, isn't it?"

"Yes, it is," Randolph replied.

"And can you clearly explain all of the above to a relatively intelligent human being in one hour—or less?"

"Yes," Randolph again agreed.

"What's most important in *this* system, Randolph—and what cannot be taught in one afternoon—is training your people to speak and listen so they can create relationships, foster friendships, grow partnerships, and develop leadership. That is what you—as a business builder and leader—must

144

train your people to do, so they can teach their people to teach their people to teach their people, and so on.

"That, my friend," he said, "is my view of a duplicatable system for success in Network Marketing. Anyone can be taught the basics of how to *do* Network Marketing in one hour on a Sunday afternoon. The rest is a process of life-long learning about *being* the very best human being you can be.

"And honestly," The Greatest Networker asked, looking intently at Randolph, "is there anything you can think of that's more important for you to learn, to get *really good at*, and then teach to other people?"

Randolph smiled and shook his head, "No, sir. I can't think of anything more important."

"Look," he said, "I told you I failed. My real failure wasn't that I wasn't being duplicatable. Truth is, I was afraid I was being all too duplicatable because my real failure was much more fundamental—and scary.

"My real failure was . . ." he paused and I just knew he was drawing us in for dramatic impact, "I didn't particularly *like people!*"

I suppose each of our faces must have looked pretty much the same—somewhere between surprise and shock—because he immediately laughed again from the very bottom of his feet, pointing at our amazed expressions.

"It's true," he said through his laughter. "And can you imagine how very hard it is to build any kind of Network Marketing business when you don't like people?"

We were silent for some time, when Nancy—bless her—said, "Tell me more about that . . . please."

He laughed again, reaching out to touch her on the shoulder. "That's great! All right, Nancy," he said with a smile followed by a sigh. "I will."

"I *taught myself* to care about people, Nancy, and I did it through Creative Listening. I won't bore you with the history of all of this, so suffice it to say that back in my early childhood I came to a conclusion about who I really was and how life really was. *Who* I was," he said matter-of-factly, yet I could feel the depth of his emotion, "was an abandoned child who would simply never be good enough—*ever*.

"That was my Listening By Default throughout my life," he said. "That was the programmed listening I had for myself—for who I thought I was.

"And *how* life was for me," he added, "was a struggle to prove I *was* good enough—good enough to love and to *be* loved—in a confused paradigm of my own creation where I couldn't and wouldn't achieve either. I have lived with that childhood decision *as if* it was the truth most of my life.

"You've heard me say that Network Marketing is all and always about relationships—yes?" he asked us, and we nodded. "So what is the source, the essence of *relationship?*"

After a thoughtful silence, Nancy was first to speak.

"Love," she said.

"Yes," he answered.

Turning to the rest of us, he continued, "And with Network Marketing being all about relationships . . . and relationships being all about love . . . we can logically deduce what we intuitively know—that Network Marketing, at its essence, is about loving and being loved.

"Dr. Watson," he said as he turned to me with a smile and a well-imitated British accent, "what do you make of *that?*"

I thought back to our ride over to the hotel that morning, finding it nearly impossible to believe it was only a few hours ago. I remembered how he asked if I could think of any reason for not being *in love* with the people you sponsored into the business. That's when I'd had the thought that *I* wasn't *good enough*. I'm not the kind of person people love, I recalled telling him.

With his encouragement, I told our group at the table about our conversation; about how he'd told me that I had made up my thoughts about not being good enough, and not being the kind of person that other people would feel love for—or feel loved by, for that matter. I told them about how he'd suggested I use affirmations to shift the balance scales in my mind in favor of new thoughts that would empower me.

"I'm fascinated," I said to him, "about this concept of early childhood decisions. Could you say more about it?"

"Sure," he replied, and sat thoughtfully looking off into the distance for a moment.

"At some time in our childhood, we come to a conclusion about how we need to live to survive in the paradigm of our lives. Are you familiar with the word 'paradigm'?"

Three of the people at the table said they were not.

"A paradigm is a model or a very specific understanding of *the way things are*. I first encountered the word back in the late '60s in a book called *The Structure of Scientific Revolutions*, written by MIT professor Thomas Kuhn.

"An example of a scientific paradigm would be Newtonian Physics. Sir Isaac—he's the guy that had an apple fall on his head and discovered gravity—had his idea of how the world worked *physically*. After the *required* initial rejection of his new idea by all the people who believed that Ol' Saint Nick Copernicus was the guy who had it right, enough other 'men of wisdom' had bought into it. Newton's *paradigm* became accepted as the way it is for life on Earth, scientifically speaking. Albert Einstein came along and upset Newton's paradigm with his work on the Theory of Relativity, which led to Quantum Physics—another new and better paradigm of how the world *really* worked.

"There's a paradigm of conventional business," The Greatest Networker said, "a paradigm of how things are bought and sold, including a Network Marketing paradigm. There is a paradigm for everything. Simply stated," he concluded, "a paradigm is the way *we say* things are.

"You and I have a 'way things are' for our lives, too. And we create that paradigm when we're children. We stick with that paradigm until something comes along to change it, simply because it is our *foundation*, which means the bottom, as in the bottom line—what all the rest is founded on."

Leaning forward on his elbows and looking at us intently, he said, "It takes a lot to change our paradigms because they're our foundation—the place we operate *from*—just like it took a lot for the world to go from Copernicus to Newton to Einstein. Hard work. I've made up my mind—*literally*—so don't confuse me with the *new* facts. We are *very* attached to the way we think things are and should be.

"You've come across people with the paradigm of 'get good grades, go to a good college, get a job with a good company, and retire in 40 years'—yes?" he asked us.

"Sure," we said. We all had.

"And then you show up with your radical new paradigm of Network Marketing: Be your own boss, have time freedom, leverage, work where you want, when you want, with whom you want, and earn enough residual income to retire in four or five years. *Ri-ight.* How'd that go over with them at first?" he asked playfully.

I could tell from the others' expressions he'd made his point.

"You all have pens and paper with you, don't you?" he asked.

I reached for mine immediately as did the others.

"Wow," he said, "I didn't even ask you to get them out, and here you all are with pens and notebooks in hand," he smiled. "Okay," he directed, "now put your pens in the hand opposite from the one you normally write with and sign your name."

As we wrote, he commented, "Awkward, isn't it? It's a whole different paradigm—surprisingly hard to do.

"It's hard work changing people's minds, too—just like having you write with your other hand. Takes some pretty strong communication, and almost always from the *outside*, to get that mind-altering job done. We usually *never* do that all by ourselves. Left to our own devices of thought, we the people don't change our minds very easily.

"But when it comes to the paradigm you find yourself in, you always have a choice," he told us. "You may accept it, reject it, or recreate it, but in order to act *with choice*," he urged, "you must first be aware that the paradigm exists and what it says about how things are.

"That's why most people—like 99.9989 percent of all the people on the planet—are not aware that their lives are being *driven* by a specific paradigm of 'the way it is' made up way back when they were children. Most of us haven't realized that the paradigm is still alive and well—defining how we live and breathe and have our being—throughout our entire adult lives."

* * *

AFTER A PAUSE and a deep breath, he turned to me. "This paradigm that you and I share—the one about not being good enough—how would that make us behave in regards to other people?"

"Well," I replied, "what I did was avoid them."

"Exactly. That's what I did my whole life," he told me. "Hey, why risk the pain of rejection—right?"

"Right," I said.

"The other thing I did—equally as dysfunctional and more openly painful," he said seriously, "was to show off. I'd be on rails to prove how brilliant I was, how creative. How worth knowing I was. Clearly *more* than good enough . . . I had to show I was *better!*

"Although you and I arrived at that early conclusion through different circumstances," he said, "we ended up in a similar place with a similar *negative* paradigm—that 'not good enough' one which had us avoid new relationships in

150

favor of being our own best friend. At best and most, we'd hang out with those few people who'd already shown us they liked or loved us—true?"

"True," I replied.

I looked back over the years recalling how I'd run from getting involved with other people, the ways that I'd stood aloof and apart from them. I recalled that I'd fed myself a series of sensible excuses for why I didn't get into relationships and how, when I did give it a try, it was often a battle struggling to show how special or smart or *something* I was so people would like me. So people—I thought—would love me.

"Can I guess from your expression," he asked me, "that you're looking back at how you've behaved, noticing how you avoided people and relationships, or set out to prove you really were good enough?"

"Yes, sir," I told him.

"Please understand," he said sincerely to the entire group, "We *made all that up*. I know that now. I just wasn't aware I'd done that—the making-up part—until I was well into my forties. I'd spent my entire life—from about four years old—as if not being good enough was the truth—who I really was. How life really was for me was that no matter how well I did—with grades, sports, art, business, money, creativity, relationships with women, you name it—it would never be *good enough*.

"Catch 22," he said, leaning back in his chair. "My child's conclusion was I wasn't good enough, so most all of everything I ever did, what drove me to accomplishment after accomplishment after accomplishment, was designed—by me—to prove that decision *wrong!* And yet I was constantly pulled back to the fact that no matter what I did, it was never good enough—like gravity, it was always pulling me down.

"Some people would call that crazy. It certainly seems schizophrenic to me. My friend and mentor, Carol McCall, prefers the more politically correct—and more compassionate—term 'dualistic.'

"Anyway," he said, moving forward to rest his elbows on the table and his chin on his folded hands, "there are many, many people today and throughout history who made the decision they weren't good enough when they were kids. It's a personal paradigm that drives athletes to championships, businessmen to become wealthy, actors and actresses to live lifestyles of the rich and famous, politicians to gain power and influence, and a number of heavy-hitting Network Marketers to build huge, successful organizations all over the world. So that paradigm has been very useful for many of us—me included.

"However," he added thoughtfully, "there is no freedom or choice in that. Living in that paradigm—unaware—is having your being, who you really are, confined in a prison of your own making.

"Remember the shepherd's story I told you?" he asked me. "Only when you become *aware*—and when you are able to bring yourself back to that awareness *in the moment*—can you lead and be led by choice. Until you do that, you will be driven by this decision of yours—a conclusion *totally made up* by the mind of a frightened little child. You will Listen By Default, you will be a paradigm prisoner, until you become aware that you have a choice."

He paused and looked at each of us in turn, his face expressionless, yet intense.

"People seem to come in two basic models in terms of this childhood conclusion which runs our lives," he continued. "Although there are as many variations on these two themes as there are individual personalities on the planet, people tend to create their fundamental paradigms wanting *quantity* or *quality*. We are either *not enough* or *not good enough*.

"A great way to discover which of these tunes a person is dancing to," he shared with us, "is to have them complete this sentence: 'No matter what I do, it's never . . .' and have them fill in the blank.

"Look at the people in your life," he encouraged us. "What are they after? Are they searching for *more* or striving for *better*? Look at your prospects. I think you'll find they'll fall into one or the other category: They want more or they want better. Their lives and work are driven by the way they think of themselves, by the paradigm of being not enough or not good enough.

"And much more important," he said, with a singular directness that had us all listening with complete attention, "look at *yourself*."

He glanced at his watch and said, "Whoa! We've gotta get back. Nancy, I hope that's enough for you. If you've got other questions, we can talk more later.

"Suffice it to say, my friends," he said, standing up from his seat, "that I learned to like people, to love and care about and for them—and to like, love, and care for *myself*. I accomplished that through Creative Listening. My teacher in much of this was Carol McCall. From my early childhood decision to what Carol calls Empowered Listening and I call Creative Listening, Open Listening, and Listening By Design, I have learned more, discovered more, and grown more through being with Carol and her work than perhaps any other teacher-coach-mentor-friend I have ever been with. I recommend her material and programs more than any others, save perhaps marriage and having—or rather being *had* by—your children," he laughed at his own turn of phrase.

"You know," he mused, "I think it would be good to start this afternoon with some more conversation about Creative Listening. I didn't really cover *how* you Listen By Design this morning.

"Good," he announced, to us—and himself. "Listening By Design, then Life Purpose. That's great! I love the way everything works out perfectly when you just trust the process," he laughed.

"Thank you for lunch," he nodded looking from face to face at each of us at the table. "I really appreciate you." He turned and walked out of the room.

Chapter Eight

By Design and On Purpose

N ANCY AND I and a couple of the others who sat with us at our lunch table walked back into the training room together. About half the group was already inside. Some of the people had taken their seats, but most were standing around in small groups talking to each other. The Greatest Networker was sitting in his tall chair on the stage, his glasses perched forward on his nose reading from his notebook, and occasionally glancing up at the audience. I noticed that a flip chart had been placed on stage. Other than that, everything was the same as it had been at the morning session.

At 1:30—I saw him check his watch, so I checked mine— The Greatest Networker reached around and turned his microphone on, clapped his hands together a number of times, and asked us all to take our seats so we could get started.

"Sit, sit, *sit*," he called out to those few people who remained standing, then added, "Welcome back. I trust lunch was both interesting and delicious," and the audience voiced agreement.

"Great. Now, your assignment over lunch was to listen—how did you do? What was the most interesting thing you discovered about listening?"

A number of people shared their discoveries, and as each person did, he asked them what "new action" they could see to take based on their discoveries.

One man, Matt, spoke about how he noticed his listening was often based in the past. The Greatest Networker asked him to say more about that.

Matt said, "I saw how, when I listened to people, my opinions were always there first. I found myself continuously thinking about whether I agreed with them or not, and I saw that all of that thinking I was doing—instead of listening—came from my past, came from what I had already decided about the person or what they were saying."

"Matt," The Greatest Networker asked, "did you find yourself listening to the conversation comparing what was being said with the way you *think* things are, or should be, kind of like seeing if there was a fit with your opinion—or not?"

"Yes," Matt replied. "I noticed that with everyone I spoke to—even with each of the other conversations I listened to but wasn't directly involved in."

"Good. Now, Matt, this will put you on the spot and I don't mean to embarrass you," The Greatest Networker said, "so I'm asking for your permission to pursue this conversation with you. I want to be very direct and honest with you—okay?"

"Okay," Matt said, adding playfully, "I won't die will I?"

"No, no. I don't think so," The Greatest Networker laughed. "At least I haven't killed anybody with a conversation, yet. But, hey, there's always a first time, Matt," he winked. "The good news is that although this conversation is pointed right at you—it's not loaded."

"Then let's go," Matt said and smiled.

"Good. Matt, you said you had already decided some things about what was being said, and you had an opinion of the person saying those things—yes?"

"Yes," Matt told him.

"Do you see how that's an example of what I called 'Reactive Listening'?" he asked.

"Sure," Matt admitted.

"Okay, why?" The Greatest Networker asked.

"Because my listening wasn't open. My opinions and judgments were in the way," Matt said, and added like a question, "Closed Listening?"

"Yes, good. Do you also see how you had Listening By Default going on there, too?"

"Yes, I think I do," Matt agreed.

The Greatest Networker climbed off his chair and walking to the front of the stage to address the entire group. "You owe Matt a thank you for *dying for our sins* here. This kind of Reactive Listening is something we all do—or is Matt the only one?" he asked with a smile. The consensus of the room was that Matt was far from alone.

"Today I want you to begin the process of moving from the habit of Reactive Listening to the choice of Creative Listening.

"Step one is Open Listening. Matt has seen how his opinions and judgments made him a Closed Listener. He couldn't

157

really *hear* the people speaking or what they were actually saying because he already had his mind made up about them. As each part of the conversation came out loud, he judged whether what was being said was right or wrong—according to him. Is this accurate, Matt?"

Matt looked down, then up and nodded, "Yes, that's right. Doesn't make me feel very good about myself."

"Join the club," The Greatest Networker quipped with a smile. "Matt, thanks for your courage in being our guinea pig this afternoon. I appreciate your willingness to take a look at yourself for us and show by your own example how we *all* do this one.

"Matt, let me know just before you think you're going to die. I promise you, in a room filled with Network Marketers, we've got a whole bunch of people who just can't wait to run right up here and *take care* of you—isn't that right, mothers?" he asked the women in the audience, who knowingly smiled and laughed.

"And for you men, how many of you are sitting there busily solving Matt's problem?" he asked with a smile.

"By nature," he told us, "women nurture, heal, and care for. Men fix, solve problems, and protect. It's just who and how we are. Comes free with the membership card in the gender club. Just Stop, Look, and Listen. Notice what you're thinking.

"If you *are* sitting there thinking 'Poor Matt,' or thinking *anything at all,* that's your Listening By Default. That's exactly what we're learning about here.

"Right now, this minute, look at your listening for Matt, for me, for this process. Look at it now, please," he requested.

After a moment—say five or ten seconds—he continued.

"Now, ask yourself this question: Does my listening—right here and right now—*empower* the people and this process, or does it *disempower* them? Ask yourself: Is my listening empowering?"

He was silent for about 20 seconds or so this time.

"You've heard me say a number of times today that we make it all up. We make up our listening. Your listening can be Reactive or Creative. It's either a habit you have or a choice you make.

"If you listen Reactively, you are listening out of *habit*. If you listen Creatively, you're listening out of *choice*. So," he asked us, "how do you want your life and work to be: *Habit* or *choice?*

"Stop, Look, and Listen," The Greatest Networker said. "Stop, look at what you're doing. A habit is something we do without conscious awareness—like tying your sneakers or brushing your teeth. Bring your awareness into play. Once you do, the habit disappears. Be creative and make up a new way to listen that empowers yourself and others. The key question is this: As long as you make up how you are listening, will you make it up to empower people—yes or no?

"This is what I mean by Listening By Design. You see, Matt is standing here being Matt. You are sitting there *listening* to Matt in a certain way, which is usually either positive or negative; either empowering or disempowering. If I listen to Matt as a jerk, does that empower him—and me?"

And he answered his own question, "Obviously, that's disempowering. The next one's a bit more tricky. If I listen to Matt as if he has a problem, which I can and should fix for

159

him . . . or as if he *needs* my help . . . or as if I've got to *rescue* him . . . or as if Matt needs my protection . . . or any of those or a hundred other disempowering ways I could listen, I am not hearing Matt with Creative Listening. I am practicing Reactive Listening; I'm Listening By Default.

"I *can be* Listening By Design simply by choosing a way to listen to Matt which empowers him. I can listen to Matt as smart. I can listen to Matt as aware. I can listen to Matt as competent. I can listen to Matt as my partner. I can listen to Matt as a leader. I can listen to Matt as special.

"I can listen to Matt in any of these ways," he told us. "All I have to do is be aware of my Reactive Listening, my Listening By Default, and make the choice to empower Matt and Listen By Design. Listen to Matt the way I choose, a way that will empower Matt and me both.

"And what do you think," he asked the people in the room, "will happen? Do you think there is a possibility that when I listen to Matt as smart, or aware, or my partner, or a leader, or as special, or as all those other positive things— that Matt will *show up* differently than if I listened to him as stupid, or asleep, or any other negative, 'reactive' thing I might be thinking?"

He sat up in his chair and remained silent for some time.

"How many of you have complainers or whiners in your downline?" he asked us.

I looked around and noticed many people saying they did, some laughing and shaking their heads.

"How many of you don't have a single complainer in your organization?" he asked.

A few hands went up.

"Interesting," he said. "Would those of you who raised your hands to say you don't have any complainers in your group stand up, please?"

About five or six people stood up.

"For all of the rest of you sitting down—and please, be *very* honest here—did any of you have a thought about these people standing now that went something like, 'Yeah, yeah, so how many people do you have in your group—two, three?' Did any of you have that thought about these people?" he asked with a smile.

A fair number of hands went up, accompanied by heads shaking, attached to a couple of pretty sheepish expressions.

"I'll tell you the truth. I've asked that question about having whiners and complainers in your network for years all around the world. Just recently—for the very first time—I asked on a coaching call if there were people who *didn't* have any of those negative people in their organization, and this one guy said he didn't. You know what my Reactive Listening was?" he asked us.

"*Right!* I went immediately to Default. I asked him—and I could hear the hint of sarcasm in my voice, 'So, how many people do you have in your group?' I fully expected him to say three or five—and all members of his Bible Study group, right?" he added with a smile.

"Well," he told us, leaning forward as if sharing something confidential, "the man answered, 'Seven thousand.'" He laughed. "*Seven thousand!* And not a whiner or complainer in the entire downline. You know why?" he asked the audience.

"Because," he answered his own question, "just like these people standing here now," he said pointing to the people who stood up, "and whether he—or any of you—knew it, know it, or not, you have a Creative Listening for your people. You have no room for complainers and whiners. You listen to your people as competent and positive. You listen to them as leaders. You listen with respect. You are Listening By Design. And because you do, *that's what shows up!*

"These people here," he said, again pointing to the six people standing, "embody Creative Listening. They are listening in a way that empowers their people *and* themselves.

"And they may do that *naturally*. They may never have had the thought that they need to Listen By Design. Empowering people may be Listening By Default for them. It happens. It's not all that common, but it happens.

"The rest of us," he continued, "like me, perhaps like you, need to *make* our listening empowered. We need to choose to use Creative Listening to bring out the best in ourselves and others—until we make *that* a habit!

"When we listen to people honoring their values, we empower them, and a great way to *know* how people are best listened to is to *ask*.

"So, Matt," he said, turning his attention back to Matt, "thanks for hanging in there with me through all of this. What ways can we listen to you that will empower you?"

"Appreciation is one," Matt said immediately. "And listen to me as smart—because I am," he added with a smile.

"What else?" The Greatest Networker asked.

Matt thought for a while, but didn't seem to come up with something right away.

"Look at your values, Matt," The Greatest Networker directed him. "What are some of your values which—when we recognize and honor them in our listening for you—would empower you?"

"Aha!" Matt exclaimed, his expression brightening with the light of discovery. "Listen to me as honest. Listen to me as a person who really makes a difference in people's lives. Someone committed to uplifting people, bringing out their best. As a leader—a servant leader."

"*Cool!*" The Greatest Networker smiled, and said to the whole room, "Can you all see and feel the shift in Matt? Do you see the difference when he's speaking about his values and how we can honor him through listening to and for his values?"

I could certainly see a difference. Even Matt's voice had changed. It sounded much stronger and more clear. I saw him as a leader and as someone committed to empowering people.

"Matt," The Greatest Networker said, "do you have a Life Purpose?"

"I'm sure I do," Matt replied.

"*Bu-ut. . . .*" The Greatest Networker prompted.

"Well, it's just not clear all the time. I'm convinced I'm here to do something important."

"Good. I'm certain you are. Would you be willing to work with me to get a first take at your Life Purpose here?"

"Sure!" Matt said enthusiastically.

The Greatest Networker invited Matt to join him up on stage, motioning him to sit in his chair. He handed him a hand-held mike and asked Matt to speak into it so we all could hear.

He moved the flip chart over next to Matt, took the cap off a red marker and quickly drew straight lines about an inch or two from the edge across the top, down the right side, across the bottom and up the left side of the paper using both hands; one holding the marker steady, the other as a guide.

"I shared with my new friends at lunch that one of my values is excellence," he told the audience. "I put a frame like this," he said, pointing to the red lines he'd drawn around the edges on the paper, "just because it adds a more finished, more professional appearance. I like it much better this way than just writing on the blank sheet. I think it's the art school background," he laughed, adding, "Gotta make those four years and all that tuition amount to something. So, Matt, tell me some of your values."

"Making a difference," Matt said immediately, and The Greatest Networker wrote 'Making a Difference' on the chart quickly, yet neatly, in block letters with a black marker.

"Great," he said. "What else?"

"Well, excellence is a value of mine, too," Matt said. "Being the best I can be—and having other people be their best, too."

"Good," The Greatest Networker said, writing both 'Excellence' and 'Being the Best/Having Others Be Their Best' on the chart.

"More," he said as he turned from writing to look at Matt.

"Leadership," Matt added.

"Good," The Greatest Networker said as he wrote. "And another?"

"Hmmm," Matt said, obviously thinking about more values. His eyes narrowed and he looked up at the ceiling.

"You mentioned honesty earlier," The Greatest Net-worker reminded him. "Is integrity a value of yours, Matt?"

"Absolutely," Matt stated firmly. "Honesty and integrity."

The Greatest Networker wrote them both down.

"You're doing really great, Matt."

"Thanks," Matt replied, obviously pleased.

"And is appreciation and recognition a value of yours?" The Greatest Networker asked with a twinkle in his eye and his voice.

Matt nodded yes, smiling, and said, "I guess so. I guess so."

"How did I know that?" The Greatest Networker said to no one in particular as he wrote Matt's words on the chart.

"Let's see what we've got, Matt," he said, and he read Matt's values out loud. "Making a Difference. Excellence. Being the Best and Having Others Be Their Best. Leadership. Honesty and Integrity. Appreciation and Recognition. Let's get about five more."

Matt's eyes narrowed and once again he looked up at the high ceiling of the hotel ballroom.

The Greatest Networker waited patiently. When more than 30 seconds had gone by, he asked Matt, "Want some help?"

"Sure," Matt said right away.

"What can you always be counted on to do, Matt?"

"Get the job done," came the immediate reply.

"No matter what?"

"*No matter what*," Matt said, and his determination was so clear I thought you could literally grab a chunk of it out of the air.

"Anything else?"

"To be fair," Matt said, and The Greatest Networker pointed to Honesty and Integrity and asked, "Is that different from these?"

"No, they're one and the same."

"Good. Let me ask you this, Matt: Who do you admire most in the world?"

"You mean like a historical figure?"

"Could be," The Greatest Networker said. "Athlete, businessperson, artist, writer, family member, actor, statesman or stateswoman, famous, not, whomever."

"Two people," Matt said. "My Mom and Michael Jordan."

"That's quite the combination," The Greatest Networker chuckled, "How's your mother at basketball?"

"No good," Matt laughed. "Couldn't sink a lay-up from a stepladder. She's five foot three."

"So tell me about these two people, Matt," The Greatest Networker urged. "What is it about them you admire most?"

"Well, Michael Jordan is the best. He's the best there ever was. He may even be the best there will ever be, but that remains to be seen, and honestly I hope he's not," Matt said. "But he was *excellence*. He didn't just play basketball *with* excellence, when he was playing, he *was* excellence itself."

"Got it," The Greatest Networker said. "And what do you admire most about that—about him, Michael Jordan?"

"Well," Matt said, "it's the excellence he brought out in others. Jordan could have been content to just be the best basketball player in the world all by himself, but he wanted more. He wanted his teammates to be their best, too. I mean, the guy had *60-point games! Sixty!* He didn't need anybody else. He *wanted* the other players to be great, too. He brought everybody's game up a notch or two—even the guys and teams he played against.

"And I think what's really special," Matt added, "is that with all the commercials and endorsements and that money stuff, he actually brought us *all* up a notch. He gave greatness a name and a face. He proved greatness was alive and kept that fact in front of the whole world. He never let us forget that there was human greatness—right there, right then."

"'I want to be like Mike,'" The Greatest Networker added.

"You bet," Matt said. "Didn't you?" he asked all of us in the room, and I was right there with him, thinking 'You bet!'

"I got it, Matt." The Greatest Networker said, paused, then asked, "And your mom?"

"My mom's the greatest. She pushed us to achieve in sports, grades, everything—my sister and I—sometimes I think she pushed *too* hard. But she loved us, and I know she did that for us."

"Can you say more about that, Matt?"

"My dad left when I was less than two, and my mom brought us up all by herself," he said. "She was my father and my mother and my best friend. She worked hard, and I know she really wanted to do her own thing—she's pretty single-minded that way. Really independent. But she set her own needs and wants aside to make sure we were taken care of first.

"She let us make our own choices, too," Matt said, "I remember her telling me if I wanted to be a garbage man, that was fine. 'Just be the *best* garbage man in town,' she said."

"Your mom sounds like a pretty incredible woman," The Greatest Networker said, placing his hand on Matt's shoulder. "What did she teach you about responsibility, Matt?"

"How to *be* responsible. I mean, she had her own friends, her own life, and she took us out with her many times. But other times, she said 'No,' to them, 'No' to doing what *she* wanted, in order to take care of us instead. I really admire her for that."

"So what is it that you admire most about her, Matt?"

"Responsibility," Matt said. "Her commitment. Her caring. And you know," he added, "she did it with a smile, too. She had fun—and she made sure we had fun, too. I know it was hard—bringing up two kids all by herself—but back then, we laughed more than anything else. She made it fun. She made me happy. She was a great teacher in so many, many ways."

"So, Matt," The Greatest Networker asked, "Is commitment a value of yours?"

"Yes."

"And responsibility?"

"Yes."

"How about having *fun?*" The Greatest Networker asked.

"Oh, absolutely!" Matt replied.

"And how about being a teacher?" he asked.

"You know," Matt said thoughtfully, "when I said that part about my mom being a great teacher, I thought about that, too. Yeah, I like that. I want to teach people how to be the best they can be."

"Matt," The Greatest Networker started to ask, after a moment's pause, "what's your Life Purpose?"

Matt turned and looked at him. I could see his eyes start to glisten. He even reached up and wiped his eyes with both his hands. Then, after a long sigh, he said, "I'm a teacher. My Life Purpose is to be a teacher."

"And what is it you will teach?" The Greatest Networker asked, his hand still on Matt's shoulder.

"I teach people how to be the best," he said. "I teach people how to take responsibility for their own greatness, to be excellent, to be the best they can be."

"And to have *fun* doing it?" The Greatest Networker asked and offered.

"*And to have fun doing it,*" Matt added and his face broke out in a huge grin that connected both his ears.

* * *

I DIDN'T WAIT to see what the rest of the people did. I started clapping and stood up immediately. And I wasn't alone. Dozens of people did the same at the same time. Soon the room was filled with a standing ovation for Matt. It was something to see. It was even better to be a part of.

The Greatest Networker stood apart and aside from Matt, smiling at him with his head lowered a little, clearly enabling Matt to soak up all our applause. Then he walked over to Matt, gave him a hug, stood back from him and said, "Thank you, Matt. You're an inspiration."

Matt jumped down off the stage, still beaming and went back to his seat.

"Okay," The Greatest Networker said, "what we're going to do now is work on getting a first take on *your* Life Purpose. Here's what I want you to do."

He had us split up into groups of six, reminding us of the conversation about synergy we'd had earlier in the day. He told us to stay with the partners we had before when we discussed values, because values were an important part of the exercise. He suggested we grab our chairs and make a series of small circles throughout the room.

Once we had our groups together, he instructed us to choose one person to write a list of about ten of his or her values. Then, he told us, highlight four or five of those values as the most important ones—and he showed us a really interesting way to do this.

He said to look over our entire list of values and find one which we would rate a ten—on a scale of one to ten, with ten being the absolute best, most important, special, for whatever reason. Which one value would we give that top score? Once we'd found that ten, he told us, rank all the others relative to that one value. Compared to the ten, what's this value worth, and that one, and that? Compared to that ten, would this one be a nine? An eight? Another ten? By ranking or rating, we'd find it easier to pick out the top four or five, he said. When we had our "essential" values, as he called them, we could weave them into a Life Purpose statement.

"There's one thing Matt did that I want to point out to all of you," he said. "When Matt spoke his Life Purpose, he began his statement with the word 'I.' That's really a great way to say it, because it has the quality of a declaration. In a sense, you're putting the world—and yourself—on notice," he told us. "You're stating 'This is the way it is, because *I said so.*'

"Given that," he added with a smile, "all you ever have to do to live your Life Purpose is *keep your word.*"

He asked us to go into our small groups, take 45 minutes to complete our list of values and write down a first take of our Life Purpose.

* * *

WHEN TIME WAS UP, he clapped his hands together a couple of times and loudly announced, "Stop there, please!

"All right," he said as we quieted down, "who wants to share their Life Purpose with us?"

I raised my hand, as did a number of others. He called on me first.

"Yes, my friend," he said, pointing to me. "Will you stand, tell everybody your first name, and state your Life Purpose, please?"

I stood, facing the group, and spoke from memory, having spent the week since our conversation in The Greatest Networker's study thinking about and refining my Life Purpose statement.

"I teach people how to be successful and free, how to achieve their Life Purposes," I said, in my best and loudest 'presentation' voice, "and I make a profound difference in millions of people's lives."

I admit I felt a little nervous at first, standing there saying that in front of all those people, almost all of whom I didn't know. But what was more apparent to me—*much* more obvious—was the physical feeling of bigness, of expansion in my chest. I also had a sense of . . . *peace.* I had the clear and compelling image in my mind that the Life Purpose I just spoke was *who I really was.*

"Thank you," The Greatest Networker said. He was smiling at me and he looked directly at me for some time. "Are you proud of yourself?"

"Yes, I am," I said full of the feeling.

"So am I," he added. "So am I. . . ."

"Who's next?" He pointed towards a tall, good-looking young man I guessed to be in his early twenties, and invited him to share his Life Purpose with the group.

"My name is Luke," he said as he stood.

"Excuse me, Luke," The Greatest Networker asked, "how old are you?"

"I'm 23," Luke said with a big grin.

"*Fantastic*," The Greatest Networker replied. "What's your Life Purpose, Luke?"

"I live with passion, playing with players, and leave a trail of joy in my path." I could tell from his beaming face how genuinely pleased Luke was with what he said, and with himself, too.

The Greatest Networker must have been just as pleased. "You're an inspiration, Luke, and I'll bet I'm not the only one in this room that wishes he or she had a Life Purpose like that when we were in our roaring twenties."

"Or had any purpose at all!" someone shouted, and we all laughed.

"Thank you very much, Luke," The Greatest Networker said. "Who's next?"

"Hi, I'm Robin," a young attractive woman stood up and said. "My Life Purpose is: I cocreate a space for healing through cooperation and partnership."

"Robin," The Greatest Networker acknowledged, "that's great. Cocreate, cooperate, partnership . . . you must be a pretty powerful partner to be in business with," he said.

"I am," Robin replied with a wide smile and sat down.

"I'm Sue," a tall, beautiful woman with hair like a lion's mane said. "I listen and dance with humanity."

"Sue," The Greatest Networker asked after a moment's pause, "tell me more about the dancing part. What do you mean by 'dance with humanity'?"

"Whatever the person I'm with is doing—what they're up to in their lives—I dance with that," she replied.

"So, like Robin, you're in partnership with people—that's the dance, yes?"

"Yes," she said.

"Sue, I take it there's a purpose to your partnership. You are dancing with people for a reason. Is that accurate?"

"Sure."

"Say more."

"I used to teach dance, and I loved helping people to move, to discover their flow," she explained. "Not just to be dancing *with* the music, but *being* the music itself. Now, I want to take that out of the dance studio and have it involve what's most important in a person's life."

"Whatever someone's dance is?" he asked.

"Yes," Sue said. "I want to partner with people, powerfully; to have what they're doing be the very best it can be—and it doesn't matter if it's fox trot, tango, jazz, tap, ballet, swing—whatever it is they're up to. I want them to experience their entire life as a dance with all the *vitality* and *grace* and *fun* and *joy* that comes with dancing your favorite dance the very best way you're capable of dancing."

"Got it!" The Greatest Networker said. "Sue, my sense is there's one more piece to your Life Purpose of 'listen and dance with humanity.' My thoughts go in the direction of two words: *Greatness* and *joy*. Would you be willing to look at that and those words and see if there's something more there you can include in your Life Purpose statement?"

"Absolutely," Sue said with a warm smile, adding, "I'll just dance with my Life Purpose—and add a little greatness and joy."

"*That's great!*" The Greatest Networker laughed. "Thank you, Sue. I appreciate you very much."

Sue sat down. and a man stood up and identified himself as Ken. "I empower excellence through freedom," he said.

"Great, Ken," The Greatest Networker acknowledged. "Thank you."

"I'm Dan," a tall fellow with glasses said as he stood, "and I lovingly guide humanity to discover the goodness of God."

Before The Greatest Networker could say anything, the woman next to Dan stood up and said, "I'm Mrs. Dan, and I empower the world to love."

"Thank you Mr. and Mrs. Dan," The Greatest Networker said.

Another man stood and said, "My name is Greg, and I serve with kindness, compassion, and love."

"*Wonderful*," The Greatest Networker said clapping his hands. "We've got a lot of love flying around this room today. Thank you, Greg."

Another tall, good-looking woman named Val stood and said, "I empower lightness of being through listening and play."

"That's just great!" The Greatest Networker said. "I'm impressed and grateful that a number of you think so much of listening to include it in your Life Purpose. Thank you. Thank *you*, Val."

A number of other people raised their hands and shared their Life Purposes, I don't recall how many. Each time someone did, I had the sensation that the room—the people in the room—were growing bigger, getting taller and actually brighter. In the past, I've usually ignored those kinds of experiences, calling them "airy-fairy," but this was *so real*. It was an amazing experience—*amazing!* I felt honored to be in that room with those people.

The last person to share was a man named Tim, who said, "I help others to heal and find joy and fulfillment through love."

The Greatest Networker thanked Tim, and sat silently for quite some time, looking down at the floor. He rubbed his eyes with both hands, and I knew he was moved by our sharing our Life Purposes. He looked up and all around the room, slowly and deliberately, as if seeing every single person's face.

"I have a question for you," he said at last, speaking softly to all the people in the room. "What would *stop you* from living your Life Purpose?"

He waited.

"Fear," someone said.

"I don't believe I can do it," said another.

"Ah, good," The Greatest Networker said, and asked, "Do you think those two—fear and belief, not believing you could do it—are pretty much the same?"

From the responses, I think most of us agreed they were.

"Okay, another question: What is your definition of belief?"

"Faith," someone in back called out.

"Knowing it's true," someone else exclaimed.

"Trust," another person replied.

"Trust in what?" The Greatest Networker asked.

"The outcome," the person said, "like, I know something's going to happen—turn out the way I hoped."

"Good," The Greatest Networker said. "So would it be fair of me to say that to believe means to know, like a fact, that something is true? That the thing will happen?"

We nodded our agreement, and I recalled our dinner together in the Japanese restaurant, wondering if he was going to put the entire room through his "most uncomfortable" exercise.

"Great," he said, and as I've come to expect, he answered my question with his next remark.

"The problem with *knowing*," he said, emphasizing the word, "is that you don't and can't *really* know anything for a fact. Everything you think you know is an interpretation. Today, even scientists realize this.

"There's a process I've used with people called 'The Most Uncomfortable Exercise in the World,' and if you don't mind," he said with a grin, "I'll spare you all *that* discomfort for today and just share with you what the exercise is like.

"How it goes," he told them, "is you state a fact and then I ask you, 'How do you know that?' When you tell me your answer, I ask you, 'How do you know *that?*' You answer again, and I ask you once again, 'How do you know *that?*'

"The exercise keeps going and going and going—like the Eveready Bunny on a bad day," he said with a laugh, and added melodramatically, "usually with your frustration *mounting* and *mounting* and *mounting*, until you exclaim with a tad of hostility directed at me, '*I don't know!*'

"My friend here," he said, pointing at me, "can attest to the level of discomfort this exercise can quickly instigate."

"I certainly can," I said loudly, a bit surprised at the passion in my voice.

He smiled at me and continued, "If your definition of belief has to do with you *knowing for a fact* that your Life Purpose *will happen* . . . that, in no uncertain terms, you'll be able to pull it off . . . that the Life Purpose you came up with here today is *who you are* and how your life *will be* from now on . . . that it's *the truth*—you're between a rock and a hard place right now, because *you cannot know that*.

"And if you can never know," he asked, "how can you ever *believe?* And if you cannot believe in yourself, in something, in anything, then how will you ever succeed?"

He paused, looking at us with that intense, yet expressionless gaze of his, then continued.

"May I offer you an empowering alternative?" he asked, rhetorically.

"What if belief did not require your *knowing anything?*"

He paused, silent.

"What if belief had nothing to do with *the truth?*"

He paused again.

"What if," he asked us with more than a hint of challenge in his voice, "what if all you had to do to have all the power and the passion of 100 percent, unshakable, totally-committed belief . . . was simply *love?*

"Yes, you heard me correctly: *Love.*"

He continued, with a deep breath, "It is my opinion that what the word *belief* really means is to *be love*.

"*Be* means to be—obviously. And *leif* comes from *leubh*, which means love. So one definition of belief you could adopt is that belief means to 'be love'—to *believe* something you would simply *be in love* with it.

"What that would mean," he said, "is in order to believe in your dreams and goals you don't have to know without a doubt they will happen. You just have to be *in love* with the idea.

"Have you ever heard someone say they believed in an- other person?" he asked. "Do you think that could simply be because they loved them? I am in love with my Life Purpose. My Life Purpose *is* who I am. I direct and empower people to live in love with excellence. That is my mission, my dream, my vision, my purpose, my passion, and the source of my per- sonal power.

"When I first began," he told us, "I did not believe—with the other meaning of the word—that I could actually live it, *be* that Life Purpose. I doubted I was good enough. But I knew I could be *in love* with the idea. That was *easy*.

"My friends," he said, getting off his chair and walking to the very front of the stage, "you don't need to know for a fact that you will accomplish your goals in order to love them— in order to be the way people are *being* when they are *in love* with life.

"Can you believe in—be in love with—your dreams?

"Can you believe in—be in love with—your aspirations?

"Can you believe in—be in love with—your Life Purpose?

"Can you believe in—be in love with—your industry, Network Marketing?

"Can you believe in—be in love with—your opportunity, your company, your products?

"Can you believe in—be in love with—*each other?*"

* * *

HE STOOD SILENTLY, looking from face to face throughout the audience. Then, with a grin that quickly became that marvelous smile of his, he added, "And can you believe, as in *be in love with* . . ." he said, looking down at his watch, "that I'm out of time?

"Thank you for having me here with you today. You're a special group of people. You are an inspiration for me, and I appreciate each and every one of you.

"Thanks," he said with a wave of his arm. He jumped down off the stage and walked up the center aisle and out of the room through the cheering standing ovation.

CHAPTER NINE

What's Next . . . ?

WE LEFT THE HOTEL shortly after The Greatest Networker finished speaking. He shook hands and exchanged hugs with the many people who came over to him and thanked him. He was gracious with all of them, yet I could see he was a bit uncomfortable. With all the attention, I thought. My sense was he would have been quite happy just to leave right away, but he stayed for them. That in itself was a lesson for me.

He spent a final moment with Ruby, thanking her and being thanked. He shook hands with Ted, gave Ruby a hug, and we were on our way.

The valet brought his car around, and I noticed he gave him a $10 tip. I thought that was a bit much, and I asked him about it.

"People like that work hard," he told me, settling into the car and snapping his seat belt, "and since I'm fortunate to have money, it pleases me to share it with other people—especially those who have less than I do. Are you familiar with the process of tithing?"

"That's where you give 10 percent of your income to the church," I replied.

"Yes, and it doesn't have to be a church, though that's one great thing to do. My friend, Randy Gage, taught me that you tithe to the source of your spiritual power. I'd known about tithing for years, but I'd never before heard it expressed the way Randy explained it. When I heard that, I asked myself: What is the source of the spiritual power in my life? My answer was *people*.

"Ever since, I've given money directly to people," he said as we pulled out of the parking lot and headed back to the highway. "Especially people who are of service to me because that's what I intend to be for others. By the way, do you know where the word tip comes from?"

"'To Insure Promptness,'" I replied, quite pleased with myself. "I heard it on a Jim Rohn tape."

"You have great taste in tapes," he said, turning to smile at me. "That's where I learned it, too," he laughed. "But doing that, giving people a tip up front, takes the Thank You out of tipping for me, so I wait until the end.

"Tell me," he asked, "what was the most interesting subject for you today?"

"Oh, there were so many," I said, straining to think of the *one* most interesting thing of all. "I don't think I can come up with only one—or even just six! It was an incredible training. My head will be spinning for days," I told him honestly.

"Well, my friend, for this day to be of real and lasting value for you, it has to contribute something to you. Can you tell me what you are taking away from today?"

"Sure," I said, even though my mind was a blank. "I'll try."

"'There is no try,'" he said in a pretty fair imitation of *Star Wars's* Master Yoda, "'Do or do not, Luke. There is no try.'"

"Okay," I laughed, "Let's see. . . ."

I told him that I'd been thinking about the new definition of belief since our dinner last Thursday night. That was a revolutionary idea for me, I said. And today I got another take on it.

"Which was . . ." he prompted.

"Love," I said. "That perhaps all we ever have to do—or *be*—in any and every situation, is love."

"Very good," he replied.

I spoke about relationship, and how I saw it now as job number one in Network Marketing.

"And in life, too?" he asked.

"In life, too," I answered.

I talked about creating relationships, growing them into friendships, offering partnership, and developing each other through leadership. He remarked that he really liked the way I put that—*offering* partnership and developing *each other*—which pleased me greatly.

I recalled the part about taking care of my body, and shared with him my commitment to treat my body as both a temple and a tool. I remembered the applause training and the genie joke, and especially all the work we did with Creative Listening.

Listening By Design was especially powerful for me, I told him. So often I found myself Listening By Default, having my past and my opinions shape what I thought and felt about people—as Matt had demonstrated. It was remarkable to realize that I have both the *responsibility* and the *power* to listen to people in ways that empower them.

"Ask, ask, ask," I said.

"Good, good, good," he responded with a chuckle.

Using the question "Where do you live?" as he did in that great conversation with Vince was something I was going to do from now on, I said.

He said it was *my* question now, and I thanked him.

What else? Stop, Look, and Listen, Commitment, Synergy—oh, that wonderful quote of Bucky Fuller's, "Sometimes I think we're alone. Sometimes I think we're not. In either case, the thought is staggering." I told him how much I loved that and that I'd had that thought myself many times looking up at the night sky.

He said he had as well.

And the whole conversation at lunch; I told him that really *fascinated* me.

He asked me to tell him more, and I did.

I thanked him for his honesty in sharing his own childhood conclusion and the mistakes he'd made when he started in Network Marketing. I remarked how it must take a lot of courage to say that kind of thing in front of strangers, such as the part about his not liking people when he started.

He told me that was true for him, at first. It was difficult, but it was easy now. He said when you experience how liberating it is to tell the truth—even and especially telling one on yourself—you get kind of addicted to the feeling of peace it brings, and the experience of freedom that comes with speaking that.

I spoke about my own thought of not being good enough, and how I suspected it of running my mind and life for years—and the lives of so many of the people who were in my life, I added.

He said that it had, and that now what there was to do was to "manage" my mind. To be aware and make choices about whether I would listen Reactively or Creatively—particularly to the "quack, quack, quack" conversation in my head.

We both laughed at that.

Oh, there was so much. Back to our lunch . . . the business of duplication—use, recommend, and sponsor—and that all we ever do is learn how to do something and then teach others what we already know how to do.

I recalled the story he'd quoted about picking up a rock and the hand being heavier and the Earth being lighter and how everything is connected and part of the balance of the whole. And that paradigm story with Stephen Covey—I told him my heart sank when he said that the father and children just came from the hospital where their mother had just died.

"I hesitate every time I think about telling that one," he said, shaking his head. "I must have told that story a hundred times and even though I *know* what's coming, I find it nearly impossible to finish it without feeling deeply saddened. I just can't help putting myself where that father was . . . or those kids. What a shock that must have been for them," he added with a deep sigh.

* **

THERE WAS MORE. Some I remembered at the time; some I honestly didn't think about again for days, even weeks. One thing I've learned in these conversations with him was not to *try* to remember anything. I haven't taken notes in years now. "If you're taking notes," he asked once, "are you *really* listening?"

"Trust the process," he always told me. "And when it comes to remembering what's important for you, trust *yourself*, because you *are* the process."

I put my pen and paper away after that.

We agreed to meet again the next Tuesday evening. He was having a small group of new leaders over for a *conversation*, and he invited me to join them. It was always a conversation with him. Life, he said, was a conversation, and now, I completely agree.

That particular night, we had what he called a Vision Party. We talked about developing Creative Tension and self-motivation, and we wrote out our visions. That one exercise alone has helped me create success for more people than I even know about!

We met again for dinner Thursday back at Hiroshi's, at my request, just he and I. He told me about win^2, and a formula for personal and professional development that harnessed geometric growth in a way that he said would have me double my abilities and competence every year for the rest of my life—guaranteed!

He was right.

We had many conversations, my mentor and I, about speaking and listening—we *always* talked about listening—and all of them were rich, rewarding experiences for me. I remember lots of stories: Doing things differently, the Emperor Moth, and the Test. I remember poems, song lyrics, and so many wonderful quotes. I will never forget them, and I'd be happy to tell you all about them.

But that's another story and another book. Or two.

Thanks for reading this one.

Read it again sometime.

I appreciate you.

About the Author

John Milton Fogg is a writer, a speaker, and a global expert on Network Marketing. He has authored and edited over 24 books and tapes which have sold over three million copies worldwide. His first book, *The Greatest Networker in the World,* has sold more than one million copies.

John is the founder and former editor-in-chief of the industry training journal *Upline®*, a former contributing editor for *SUCCESS* magazine and the founding editor-in-chief of *Network Marketing Lifestyles* magazine.

He has spoken across the United States, Canada, Australia, Korea, New Zealand, Taiwan, Malaysia, Singapore, and Russia. His books and articles have been translated into Chinese, French, German, Hebrew, Hungarian, Italian, Korean, Portuguese, Russian, and Spanish.

John is the director of The Greatest Networker Mentor Program, a six-month international coaching course for Network Marketing leaders.

You can learn more about John and all he is doing on the Internet at www.GreatestNetworker.com.

John lives with his wife, Susan, and their two children, Rachel and Johnny, in the foothills of the Blue Ridge mountains outside Charlottesville, Virginia.